D1388039

QUIET PLEASE

By the same author

Four-iron in the Soul
No News at Throat Lake
California Dreaming: A Smooth-running
Low-mileage, Cut-price American Adventure

QUIET PLEASE

A Ryder Cup Story with a Twist

Lawrence Donegan

YELLOW JERSEY PRESS
LONDON

Published by Yellow Jersey Press 2003

2 4 6 8 10 9 7 5 3 1

Copyright © Lawrence Donegan 2003

First published in Great Britain in 2003 by
Yellow Jersey Press

Random House, 20 Vauxhall Bridge Road,
London SW1V 2SA

Random House Australia (Pty) Limited
20 Alfred Street, Milsons Point, Sydney,
New South Wales 2061, Australia

Random House New Zealand Limited
18 Poland Road, Glenfield,
Auckland 10, New Zealand

Random House (Pty) Limited
Endulini, 5A Jubilee Road, Parktown 2193,
South Africa

The Random House Group Limited Reg. No. 954009
www.randomhouse.co.uk

A CIP catalogue record for this book
is available from the British Library

ISBN 0–224–06112–7

Papers used by Random House are natural, recyclable
products made from wood grown in sustainable forests.
The manufacturing processes conform to the environmental
regulations of the country of origin

Typeset by SX Composing DTP, Rayleigh, Essex
Printed and bound in Great Britain by
William Clowes Limited, Beccles

To golf marshals everywhere

Thanks to:

Jonny Geller, Douglas Kean, Tristan Jones, Rachel Cugnoni, John Huggan, Richard Williams, Tom Jenkins and Maggie Shiels, as well as a few other people who'd get into trouble if I mentioned their names here. You know who you are, and thanks. Most especially, thanks to all the marshals at the 2002 Ryder Cup, all of whom helped make the experience memorable.

QUIET PLEASE

Getting There

IF YOU ARE THE KIND OF UNSERIOUS PERSON who spends time thinking about which is the world's greatest golf tournament, and I'm duty bound to tell you that's exactly the kind of person I am, then there is only one serious candidate. It's more joyous than the US Open, and its Calvinist obsession with defending par. It's more historic than the US PGA Championship, a tournament that has been won by several golfers who could accurately, if unkindly, be called obscure. As for the event held annually at Augusta, Georgia, tell me this – what's so great about flowerbeds and misogyny? Sure, the Open Championship has tradition and history, as well as other attractions that appeal to a Scotsman like me

– day trips to the seaside, terrible weather, rows and rows of food stalls selling chips. But not even the Open can compare with the greatest golf tournament in the world.

I am of course referring to the Ryder Cup.

The Ryder Cup is golf distilled to its rawest competitive essence. Twelve of the best European players against twelve of the best Americans. Eight fourball matches, eight foursomes and twelve singles. Three days of golf during which every single swing made by every single player counts for something. Twenty-eight matches – all of them akin to the final pairing on the final day of a Major championship.

There's a photograph of Sergio Garcia and Jesper Parnevik taken seconds after the latter had just holed a chip shot during the 1999 Ryder Cup at Brookline. They are dancing towards each other, arms aloft, legs askew, faces contorted with what must be joy but could easily be mistaken for excruciating pain. They look like the punchline in one of those old good news/bad news jokes. The good news is they've just won £10 million on the lottery. The bad is news is Sergio's pants are on fire and Jesper forgot to bring a pail of water.

I'm no better myself. Come Ryder Cup time, my behaviour becomes equally erratic – one part anti-social to two parts slobbering, patriotic fool.

Take the 1999 match at Brookline, won by the Americans after an epic final day's singles. For three days, I took the phone off the hook and parked myself in front of a television set, refusing to leave my seat except to give the nearest warm body a congratulatory bear hug whenever a European player holed a putt. Not since *Our Friends in the North* had there been such drama. Not since Diana told *Panorama* the monarchy was doomed had I been so ecstatic. Not since she turned out to be wrong had I been so crushed.

I have watched eight Ryder Cup matches. It is the best television show on earth. Yet for me, a golf fanatic so extreme I once gave up a job on the best newspaper on the planet to caddy for the world's 438th best professional golfer, it had only ever been a television show.

'I would give anything to be at the Ryder Cup,' David Duval once said. Thank you, David. You took the words right out of my mouth. I would give anything to be at the Ryder Cup. To see it with my own eyes. To smell it, touch it. To listen to it without Peter Alliss droning on in the foreground about his dear old friend Wing Commander Bertie Truffel-Jacket and the chaps back in the spike bar at the Royal Mid-Surrey Golf Club.

I would give anything to be at the Ryder Cup. The question, one I faced as 29 September 2002 approached, was how to achieve my goal?

The most glamorous route would have been the one taken by Garcia and Parnevik. I could somehow be selected for the European team. Think about it: free golf at a decent course, free food, free accommodation – I might even get to share bunk beds with Colin Montgomerie! – free clothes and all the public adulation I could handle. Alas, I am a high handicap golfer. I have broken 80 for eighteen holes once in my life but only because I didn't count the bad shots. The last time I checked I wasn't even a member of the European Tour Order of Merit, far less one of ten players who had won enough prize money to earn automatic selection.

Being one of the two captain's picks was a more realistic option, although only in the way that being invited to conduct the Berlin Philharmonic with a Sainsbury's baguette was a realistic option. But wait – I had *contacts*. I once sat next to Sam Torrance, Europe's captain, on a bus in Morocco; he in the window seat, me on the aisle. We were going from the hotel to the golf course and struck up a conversation as we pulled into the car park at the Royal Dar es-Salaam golf club.

'Can you let me past, mate, I'm late for my tee time,' he said.

'No problem,' I replied.

'Thanks.'

I pondered for a while whether or not I could parlay this admittedly brief exchange into one of the most sensational sports stories of this or any other decade — TORRANCE STUNS GOLF WORLD: PICKS UNKNOWN HACKER TO PLAY IN RYDER CUP — before concluding my energy would be more efficiently spent pursuing more achievable goals. There was Real Madrid to play for, Cameron Diaz to have rampant (but also very tender and loving) sex with and the first great Scottish novel of the 21st century to write.

I convinced myself there was no way I was going to the Ryder Cup. But as the appointed day at the Belfry drew ever closer, my desire to be there in person only intensified. I thought of other scams.

There was always caddying. *Of course there was.* I could caddy at the Ryder Cup. As I said before, I had been a caddy on the European Tour and even though I don't like to boast, with a little more time and practice (say around a hundred years' worth) I could have been brilliant at the job, regardless of what my erstwhile employer told the *Sunday Times* newspaper after we went our separate ways and I wrote a book about the experience. '[He] was a pain in the arse . . . and not a very good caddy for me,' he said. This sounds harsh but was in fact a gross distortion of what he actually said, which was: 'Some people might say he was a pain in the arse but I couldn't possibly comment . . . he wasn't a very good caddy for me but I'm sure he would have been perfect for Tiger Woods.'

I blame Rupert Murdoch for the misunderstanding. Either him, or a faulty tape recorder.

Luckily, there are a handful of people on the professional golf circuit who aren't taken in by scurrilous media gossip and at least one of them is a friend. I say friend when perhaps I should say 'a professional golfer to whom I say "hello" and who at least acknowledges I exist by saying "hello" back'. Not that I am a name-dropper but his name is Lee Westwood. You may have heard of him: winner of twenty tournaments around the world, former number one golfer in Europe; member of three Ryder Cup teams, including Sam Torrance's 2002 squad.

Back when I was a caddy I had the privilege of being in the same group as Westwood for a round during a tournament in Germany. He shot 65, although he played so brilliantly it could have been 55. I'd seen him on a few occasions since then and each time I sought to ingratiate myself by telling him his was the best round of golf I had ever seen. 'Did I shoot a 65 in a tournament in Germany? I can't remember that one,' he usually replied.

This was impressive in one way – how good a golfer must one be to forget shooting a 65? – but in another offered me a golden opportunity, especially in my current dilemma. If Lee Westwood couldn't remember the best round of golf I had ever seen then he probably couldn't remember that while he was shooting 65 at the Gut Kaden Golf Club near Hamburg in June 1996 I was entirely responsible for my player almost missing the cut; that I couldn't select the right clubs, couldn't read putts and didn't know the rules of golf.

It was a long shot – a faded driver out of the

rough across a crocodile-infested ocean to a green the size of George W. Bush's brain, so to speak – but in my desperation to be at the 2002 Ryder Cup I convinced myself that somehow Westwood would let me caddy for him at the Belfry.

As luck would have it, three weeks before the tournament was due to start I was sent to Seattle by a magazine to cover the World Championship of Golf. My assignment was to interview Colin Montgomerie but my goal was to find Lee Westwood.

It took me an hour to track him down. He was hurrying out of the clubhouse.

'Hi, Lee, how's tricks?' I said with an obsequious smile.

He scanned my face like it was a large and unexpected tax bill before the light of recognition flickered on. 'All right, mate, what are you doing here?'

'Interviewing Monty,' I said.

He smiled and kept walking. 'Good luck.'

A few weeks earlier Montgomerie, astonished and upset that the press had had the temerity to say he was moody, went into one of his moods and announced he'd 'had enough'. Enough of what, no one was quite sure; the press, life, waking up in the morning with red hair? Anyway, I had been granted the privilege by his management company of being the first journalist to interview him since his outburst.

'I'll probably need it,' I laughed. 'Anyway, the thing is, Lee, I wanted to ask you something.'

Westwood didn't break stride. 'What is it? It'd better be quick, I'm going to be late for my tee time.'

Just then I noticed his caddy walking behind him. It was Davie Renwick. The *great* Davie Renwick. One of the most important lessons I learned during my time on tour was that professional golf caddies operate within a strict social hierarchy that encourages successful caddies like Renwick – who had caddied three different players to victory in Major championships – to treat unsuccessful caddies like me as if they were something unpleasant they'd found in a caddyshack burger.

It was to Davie's great credit that he couldn't be bothered with all that nonsense and always did me the honour of acknowledging my humble presence, even giving me some advice whenever he saw me stumbling around the golf course.

'Aw' right, big man. Long time no see,' he said.

'Davie,' I replied sheepishly, and as I shook the hand that passed the four-iron to Jose Maria Olazabal on the fifteenth at Augusta on that triumphant day back in 1994 a simple truth hit me on the bridge of the nose like a well-aimed punch from Lennox Lewis: I wasn't fit to carry Davie Renwick's travel bag to the Ryder Cup, never mind carry his boss's golf bag during it. Davie made more money carrying golf clubs than half the players on the European Tour had made swinging them. Not only had he forgotten more about caddying than I could ever hope to learn, he had forgotten everything I *had* learned because it wasn't worth knowing.

Get real, Lawrence, the voice of reason in my head whispered. For once, even I had to agree. Lee Westwood would no more fire Davie Renwick and employ me than he would turn up for the Friday morning fourballs at the Belfry dressed as the back end of a pantomime horse.

We scampered to the tee, the three of us. Davie and I watched Westwood take a couple of practice swings with a two-iron and then hit his ball straight left into the redwood trees lining the fairway. I'm sure I had seen a worse shot by a professional golfer but at that moment I couldn't quite recall when. Renwick looked impassive. Westwood bent down, picked up his tee and then walked over to the bag.

'What was it you were after?' he sighed.

What I was after no longer existed. It was just a ridiculous dream and I'd woken up.

I scrambled for something sensible to say but in the end I settled for something tactless.

'Oh it was nothing really, Lee. I was just wondering – how is your game these days?'

'Oh, it's absolutely terrific, can't you tell?' he said, sliding the offending club into the bag before stomping off up the fairway.

If you ask me, the problem with professional golfers these days is not that they are too rich or too pampered or that they dress like Mormons on casual Friday. It's that they're far too sensitive.

I know what you're thinking. You're thinking what my girlfriend was thinking at breakfast the week before the Ryder Cup started and I had a day planner spread out across the kitchen table, trying to figure out when I could fit in some work between watching seventeen hours of golf on television every day.

'Why didn't you just buy a ticket like everyone else and go as a spectator?' she said with her usual charming naïvety.

'I'm glad you asked me that,' I said and, truly, I was.

Serious people have strong views on global

politics and the future of narrative fiction in a post-postmodern world where people have the attention span of an amoeba. I have strong views about the maltreatment of the general public at golf tournaments.

Why didn't I just buy a ticket for the Ryder Cup? Please let me explain. For one thing they cost, I believe, £80 a day. For another, they were sold out, or least someone told me they were. In any case, I'd twice paid to watch big-time golf tournaments and both times it occurred to me after about ten minutes that rather than me paying the organisers for the privilege of watching, they should be paying me for putting up with the indignity of being treated like a Jersey calf on a cross-Channel ferry. Sure, I wanted to see the Ryder Cup with my own eyes, to smell it, hear it and touch it, but not while standing behind fifteen rows of people, half of them with handheld periscopes and the other half with umbrellas.

'. . . Plus the food they sell to spectators at golf tournaments is disgusting and expensive, the car parking is, like, a half-marathon away from the golf course and it's always knee-high in mud and then when you finally make it on to the course they've got these idiots – marshals, they're called – who wear these stupid little armbands and think they're the masters of the universe. If there's a spot where you can get a really good view of the golf, trust me, these Nazis will tell you to move and then when you do move they grab the really good spot for themselves. Of course, if you argue with them they shove this stupid little sign that says "Quiet Please" right in your face, and you know the really irritating thing? These bastards haven't even bought a ticket, they get in for nothing . . .'

There was more to say on the subject, so much more, but before I could fully get into my stride my girlfriend got up and walked to the other end of the house, ostensibly to look for the newspaper but really, I think, because her ears were about to start bleeding.

'Then why the bloody hell don't you get a job as a marshal?' she said, coming back into the kitchen with a newspaper under her arm.

'Who, me? Don't be so ridiculous. How can I get a job as a marshal?'

'Oh yes, silly me. I forgot,' she sighed. 'Only certified geniuses need apply for the taxing job of wearing an armband and holding up a "Quiet Please" sign. That rules you out.'

She can be very sarcastic when she puts her mind to it.

'Very droll. Have you ever thought of writing jokes for Bob Hope? I hear he's planning a farewell tour.'

'Oh sorry for being so stupid,' she sighed. 'I thought you said marshals don't pay to get in and they get all the best views. So I'll ask again: why don't you get a job as a marshal?'

'Because it's . . . because it's . . .' Because it was an inspired idea and I couldn't believe I hadn't thought of it myself, was the correct answer, but in the circumstances it wasn't one I was prepared to concede. 'Because it's a stupid idea.'

'Whatever, dude,' she said, then started to read her newspaper.

She's a wonderful woman, my girlfriend, but she's never been the same since she bought that Eminem CD.

Here's how you get a job as a marshal at the world's greatest golf tournament. Three days before it is about to start you call the office of the organisation running the event and say you understand there's a tournament going on at the Belfry later in the week and that, if someone asks you nicely, you would consider volunteering for marshalling duty. Once the person at the other end of the phone has clambered off his high horse, you will then be given a lecture about the threat of global terrorism and about how Tom, Dick and Harry can't just expect to call on the eve of a major international sporting event and expect to walk on to the highly trained 'security team'; there are procedures to follow, vettings to be carried out and all sorts of other details – top secret details that can't be given out over the phone – that exist for the sole purpose of making the person delivering the lecture seem very important and making you seem very stupid and insignificant. You can stay on the phone listening to this lecture if you like. Personally, I gave up when I was told if I wanted to apply for marshalling duties at the 2006 Ryder Cup in Ireland my interest would be noted and passed on to the appropriate authorities for consideration.

Put the receiver down. It's time for a break. Have a drink of water, take two strong painkillers and ponder awhile on the pivotal role of the jobsworth in the decline of the British Empire.

Once your headache has eased, you then call the golf course that is hosting the event. There, a very nice woman with a voice with the texture of warm honey will tell you she isn't quite sure who is in charge of marshalling but if you hold on please she'll find out and put you through. Eventually, you will be transferred to another very nice woman who tells you it's nothing to do with her but, hang on a moment, she thinks she knows who you should speak to. Eventually, and when I say eventually I mean half an hour later, you will be connected to an answering machine telling you the greenskeeping staff are all out trimming the fairways but please leave a message. This will happen four or five times. Don't let it worry you. This is Britain in the 21st century; it's meant to be a shambles.

Finally, and only if you are one of those lucky people who wins lotteries or falls in the Thames and swims ashore with a lightly grilled lobster between their teeth, you will call and someone will pick up the phone and say the magic words: 'Marshals' office, can I help?'

At this stage, you'll think there's no point in making a simple request to become a marshal at the Ryder Cup. The temptation is to invent some ridiculous story in the hope that they'll break the rules and give you the job. Go ahead. If lying gives you the kind of groovy high you've missed since selling your Grateful Dead albums, go ahead and make stuff up. Tell the person on the other end of the phone you're a professor of golfology at

Harvard University and you're working on the definitive history of crowd control. Tell him you're terminally ill but before you die you'd like to get Stewart Cink's autograph. Tell him you've got £5,000 in a brown envelope. Tell him any old rubbish you like, it won't make any difference.

'Sorry, mate. I'm not the boss or anything but as far as I know they stopped taking volunteers for marshalling about two years ago,' the friendly voice on the other end of the line will say. 'Now if you'll excuse me I've got to go. My bacon roll is getting cold.'

You will want to give up. I don't blame you. You've spent the last ten hours speaking to people whose sole purpose for being on this earth is to frustrate you. Your spirit is broken. You hate the world. The phone bill is going to come to about three hundred quid. Of course you want to give up, but take my advice: don't. Success is closer than you think. Call back. Call back because two minutes later an angel with a London accent will answer, and when she does all you have to do is ask her a straight question. It's that easy. Just say: 'Any chance of marshalling at the Ryder Cup? I'm a golf fanatic and I really want to be there.'

'Of course you can, love,' she'll reply. 'We could do with some extra help around this place. See you tomorrow morning. How does seven o'clock sound?'

It sounded like a time of the day I hadn't seen for at least five years but I wasn't going to tell her that, was I?

Practice Day

A MOMENT OF SYMPATHY, PLEASE, FOR Sylvanus P. Jermain, whom history records as a benefactor of public parks in his home town of Toledo, Ohio, when really his contribution to the forces which shape the modern world – and the modern sporting world in particular – is a little more newsworthy than that. The Ryder Cup was his idea. Sort of.

In 1920, Jermain, a friend of several of America's leading players and a member of the very swanky Inverness Golf Club – which was hosting that year's US Open – suggested a match between the best golfers from either side of the Atlantic. He garnered support from, among others, Walter Hagen, then the best player in America. A magazine called

Golf Illustrated started raising money to send a team across the Atlantic, but when its efforts came up short, supporters of the match went begging to the US PGA.

Despite the best efforts of the Association's out-going president John Mackie – who described the idea as a scam dreamed up by a few golf professionals looking to get a free trip to Britain – the Association agreed to pay each player $1,000 expenses.

Jermain's brainchild came to fruition the following year at Gleneagles, Scotland.

To describe this first annual transatlantic challenge match as a gigantic flop would be a serious misuse of the English language. Let's just say it was the Millennium Dome of its era. For a start, Gleneagles hotel was still under construction, which meant the American visitors had to stay in a railway carriage in Auchtermuchty. And for another three things, no one came to watch, the course was an unkempt shambles and the match itself was a one-sided bore. If you really want to know, Great Britain won 9–3. Meanwhile,

Sylvanus P. Jermain returned to obscurity, from where he continued his campaign to make sure Toledo, Ohio, had the best public parks this side of, well, Akron, Ohio.

However, the idea of an annual Anglo-American golf match was not dead. Six years later, a seed merchant from St Albans called Samuel Ryder was in the bar at Wentworth Golf Club after an enjoyable day spent watching an unofficial match between American and British golf professionals. It's not known how much alcohol had been consumed but it is generally acknowledged that at some stage in the proceedings Ryder announced, 'We really must do this again' and that he'd provide the cash to buy a cup.

One year later, at Worcester Country Club, Massachusetts, they did do it again.

America won the first official Ryder Cup. America won seventeen of the next twenty-one Ryder Cups, including all ten that were staged in the USA. Two of the three British victories came during the tournament's formative years, when no one took the event that seriously. Only at Lindrick Golf Club, Yorkshire, in 1957, when the Americans were under the perfectly understandable impression that all they needed to do to win was turn up, did the British manage to sneak out a victory.

It was another twelve years, at Royal Birkdale in 1969, before we came close again. That was the year Jack Nicklaus won plaudits from golf fans around the world – and dog's abuse from a few of his team-mates – for conceding a four-foot putt on the last hole of his deciding singles match against Tony Jacklin which allowed the British team to halve the match.

Nicklaus's charity extended beyond the eighteenth green at Royal Birkdale. Off the course, he was at the forefront of those lobbying for the rules to be changed in order to give the British at least a fighting chance of winning. One suggestion – to have the Americans play with a pair of live scorpions shoved down the back of their boxer shorts – was immediately dismissed. Others, such as expanding the British team to include players from Ireland, were adopted. When that didn't work and America kept on winning it was decided to expand the Great Britain and Ireland team to include European players.

This is where it starts to get interesting – at least it does for those of us who think Seve Ballesteros is the best Ryder Cup player ever.

Not that the great Spaniard made an immediate impact. For instance, at the Greenbrier Golf Club, West Virginia, in 1979, he lost four of his first five Ryder Cup matches. Two years later he refused to play after a row about appearance money. Without him, Europe was hammered. With him, Europe would still have been hammered, because as anyone who knows anything about the history of the Ryder Cup (and even those who, like me, know the bare minimum) will tell you, the 1981 American team – Nicklaus, Watson, Kite, Trevino et al. – was the greatest the competition has ever seen. The Yanks won eighteen and a half to nine and a half at Walton Heath.

Fortunately, in 1983 Ballesteros was persuaded to play by Europe's new captain, Tony Jacklin. That year, despite being forced to step on to the course in some of the worst golf outfits ever assembled – scarlet trousers with a white belt, with non-matching blue and white striped polo shirt! – a European team inspired by the Spaniard came within one point of winning the Cup in America for the first time ever.

The balance of power had shifted.

Europe won four of the next eight tournaments and halved another. Ballesteros made his last appearance as a player in 1995, at Oak Hill Country Club, New York, when his game had deteriorated to the point where he could barely get the ball off the tee. But by sheer force of will he still managed to spur his teammates on to victory. He won as captain two years later at Valderrama, then took his leave of an event he had transformed.

I won't dwell too long on the 1999 event at Brookline, not least because as a biased European the memories are too painful. In any case, who wants to know my opinion about the infamous incident on the seventeenth green when Prince Andrew lookalike Justin Leonard holed a fifty-footer and his team-mates decided it was a perfect time to stomp up and down the line of Jose Maria Olazabal's putt? Let's just say that since that torturous Sunday afternoon hardly a day has passed when I haven't felt like stomping up and down Justin Leonard's spine.

Given that this was out of the question, I settled for counting the days until September 2001, when the European team would get its chance for revenge. If that's how I – a mere spectator – felt, God only knows what the players were thinking.

The terrorist attacks of September 11 caused the postponement of the 2001 match. The event was rescheduled for September 2002, at the same venue, the Belfry, with the same captains – Sam Torrance and Curtis Strange – and the same teams.

I thought this was a terrific idea both because – in its own small way – it was a fitting tribute to those who died in New York, Washington and Pennsylvania and because it was only fair that the players who had earned their way on to the 2001 teams should have those efforts recognised. This was especially true for the likes of Paul McGinley, Niclas Fasth, Pierre Fulke and Phillip Price – 'fringe' players who might never make the team again.

The win-at-all-costs brigade in Europe insisted Torrance should have used the delay as an excuse to dump those four and replace them with better players. To his eternal credit, Europe's captain dismissed the suggestion out of hand. Strange did likewise, even though it meant he was landed with at least one player from his original 2001 team – Hal Sutton – who was so badly out of form he might have been pushed to give me a decent game over eighteen holes. Both teams were at an equal 'disadvantage'.

Actually, if you ask me it hardly matters any more who is picked to play. Such is the tension that surrounds the matches, it has become what some of my less cultured American friends like to describe as a 'crap shoot'. Anyone can win over eighteen holes, regardless of their reputation or who they are playing against. Just ask Tiger Woods, whose record in his two appearances before the 2002 cup was won three, lost five, halved one.

Sure, Curtis Strange's team was the favourite with the bookies this time round but, frankly, as the great day approached the only guarantees were that the match was going to be close and that I was going to have the sporting experience of a lifetime.

That's why I couldn't wait to get there.

Understandably, the year-long delay had thrown some of the organisation into disarray. Being an understanding soul, I was prepared to forgive the roadworks on the M42. The lack of clues as to where the tournament was taking place was less forgivable, especially as I'd never been to the Belfry before. Not one road sign, not one helpful policeman, not even a traffic cone, except on the M42 of course, where Steven Spielberg was filming *Invasion of the Traffic Cones*.

I drove round and round the outskirts of Tamworth for half an hour, watching the sun rise over the A5 to God Knows Where.

It may have been intuition but after my second visit to the petrol station to the west of the town, the one with the bouncy castle in the forecourt and *Bouncy Breasts Monthly* in the magazine rack, I selected from a choice of seven roundabouts, veered left down the first exit and drove south for five miles.

And there it was, the Belfry. And there it was, the official Ryder Cup car park. And there he was, Britain's most objectionable car park attendant.

'You can't park in there,' he shouted from the middle of the road, hand raised, face set defiantly, a less sympathetic version of the hero who stopped the tanks rolling in Tiananmen Square. I was half minded to keep driving, but given that an attempted murder charge would have undone all my good work in getting this far, I drew to a gentle halt and stuck my head out of the window.

'Hi there, how are we today?' I said, cheerily.

'I said, you can't park there.'

'Fantastic,' I smiled. 'I'm doing very well too, since you ask.'

'No one parks here without a pass.'

'Yes, I know that because even though we've only just met you've already told me twice. That's why as soon as I get to the marshals' headquarters I'm going to get a marshal's parking pass, come straight back here and hang it on my rear-view mirror and then your life can return to the sweet equilibrium it so richly deserves,' I said. Or words to that effect.

'Sorry. No members of the public. Official event staff only.'

'But I'm not a member of the public, I'm a marshal.'

'Well, if you're a marshal, can I see your parking pass?'

'You could if you'd give me five minutes to go inside and pick it up.'

'Sorry, mate, no can do.'

'Please.'

He shrugged that shrug, you know, the don't-mess-with-me-I'm-wearing-an-official-issue-donkey-jacket shrug they teach on day one at car park attendant school.

'But how am I going to get a parking pass if you won't let me park my car here until I go inside and pick one up?' I said, with uncharacteristic restraint.

'Not my problem. All I'm doing is sticking to the rules. If you've got any complaints, you'll have to take them up with someone else.'

'Who do you suggest? Ms Dynamite? The pope? The Prime Minister of Finland?'

This was absolutely the wrong approach, not least because it introduced a kind of behavioural equivalence into our relationship. Before, he was a jumped-up, unhelpful little man who, judging by the obvious pleasure he derived from bossing people around, had lived a very meaningless life (possibly alone in a bedsit in Tamworth with nothing for company but a 12-inch TV set and a pile of pornographic magazines), and I was a charming, James-Stewart-goes-to-the-Ryder-Cup figure. Now we were just two supercilious prats locked in a battle of wills, a battle I had no chance of winning because, as I've already mentioned, he was wearing the donkey jacket of authority.

I could see victory in his smile. 'Could you please move over to the side. There's someone trying to get past,' he said, motioning the car behind me to come forward. 'Someone with a parking pass.'

I tried to drive round him. He danced in front of my bumper like an incompetent goalkeeper getting ready to face a penalty. I edged forward. He shouted over to another attendant, who radioed for a copper, who arrived just in time to stop either me hitting him or (a more likely occurrence because I haven't thrown a punch in anger for twenty-seven years) him hitting me. The policeman, a

Solomon-esque figure as it turned out, listened carefully while I explained the problem, then shot the attendant a look of weary disbelief and told me to go and park my car.

In keeping with the theme of the morning, the marshals' headquarters wasn't signposted. I followed the stream of people heading to the far end of the golf course. Some of them had handheld signs which said 'Quiet Please', others had rucksacks, a few were carrying those clever canvas chairs that fold away to the size of a cigarette packet. All of them were wearing black trousers, red waterproof tops and black shoes. In stark contrast to me. I was wearing jeans, a pair of Nikes and a grey hooded top with a BETTY'S GENTLEMEN'S CLUB logo. (In my defence, I've never been to Betty's Gentlemen's Club. I bought the top in a secondhand store in Santa Barbara, California.)

Eventually, we arrived at a quadrangle of tents and Portakabins next to the practice driving range. This was Marshal HQ.

I stood around for a while, watching people come and go. The ones who were coming and going tended to be younger and more excited. They were slipping orange armbands on to their sleeves. A handful remained, mostly older men who were wearing different-coloured armbands spelling out their position in what was clearly a very complicated hierarchy: senior marshal, deputy assistant chief marshal, deputy senior assistant chief marshal, and so endlessly on. Above even this exalted group there were others who didn't have armbands but handheld radios into which they were constantly talking.

'Carl, are you there, Carl? Roger here. Roger and out.'

'Yes, Roger, Carl here. Roger and out.'

'Roger, Carl. Why am I talking to you on a walkie-talkie when you're only standing five yards away? Is it because my life, my entire self-worth, has been invested in this fifty-quid electronic device? Roger. Roger and out.'

'Copy, Roger. Probably. Me too. Roger and out.'

I shouldn't make fun, because the handheld radio brigade were very friendly and kept asking me if there was anything they could do to help me. I told them I was looking for the chief marshal.

'Carl, Roger here. Copy. Where's Barry? Copy.'

'Roger, Roger. He's over there . . .' Carl, who was standing five yards away, pointed at a Portakabin where a group of men were seated round a table discussing the future of the internet or something equally important, judging by the gravity of their expressions: '. . . he's in a meeting with the generals.'

The generals, Roger explained, were the most senior marshals. You could tell who they were because they wore black water-proof tops and were so important they didn't need a walkie-talkie. The generals, he snorted, held meetings more or less con-tinuously, except when they broke off to hold a meeting about meetings.

Another half-hour passed before the generals' meeting finally ended. The chief marshal was the last man out of the Portakabin. I introduced myself.

'Hello, pal. What can I do for you?' he said.

Barry's demeanour was remarkably calm for a man charged with the responsibility of ensuring good order at an event which had become known as much for its attendant rowdiness as its golf. There was also the problem of tackling the threat of terrorism, although this wasn't the responsibility of the marshals, I was pleased to discover. Coming into the Belfry, I'd noticed police officers everywhere, many of them carrying guns.

'Are you the guy from the magazine?' Barry said after I finished my story.

Ah, yes.

Did I mention my magazine story? I say magazine story, it was more of a magazine lie. I'd concocted it when the woman I'd spoken to the day before called me back to say she'd made a mistake, that it wouldn't be possible for me to become a Ryder Cup marshal at such short notice. I'm ashamed to say I then told her I was from a fantastically well-known magazine which I won't name here because one day I hope to work for it and presumably the editor has rules about not employing people who impersonate its journalists in order to gain entry to major sporting events. I'm not proud of myself, but the point is it worked. Try it yourself but make sure your 'assignment' has at least an air of plausibility. Don't, for instance, turn up at the gates of Wimbledon and tell them you're from the *Angling Times*.

'That's right, I'm the guy from the magazine,' I said, sincerely.

'Hang on,' he said, then disappeared into one of the tents and came back with an orange armband. 'Take this and get yourself over to the tenth tee for eight o'clock. And by the way, the hooded top isn't going to work. Go over to the tent there and they'll give you some marshal gear. And you'll need to get yourself some black trousers.'

The tenth tee. My heart started dancing the fandango. I'd been handed a prime assignment.

The spasms of ecstasy eased slightly as a woman at the tent started rummaging around in boxes to find clothing for me. I don't want to sound ungrateful, especially as it was free, but it was disgusting. There were two red T-shirts, a black cap, a red waterproof top and what may have been a tank top (though I'm not quite sure because my fashion vocabulary only dates back to 1978).

'The T-shirts say large but they're bigger than large,' the woman said.

I opened out one of the T-shirts. It was bigger than Somerset.

'Thanks,' I lied. 'When can I hand them back in?'

'No, no, they're yours to keep. It's the only perk of the job,' she said.

'Can't I hand them back, please?'

She seemed puzzled. 'You could, but no one will be here to take them off you. Is there something wrong with them?'

I shook my head, thanked her and headed out across the golf course towards the tenth tee, detouring momentarily into a portable toilet, where I stuffed the tank top and the cap into one of the chemical loos.

It was only a practice day but already there were hundreds of spectators coming through the gates. Many were already lining the fairways and filling the grandstand behind the eighteenth hole. A group of marshals had gathered by the tenth tee, dressed uniformly in red and black, like a wedding party outside the church of some weird religious sect. The mood was quiet but excited.

'We got the best spot,' whispered one man in a gleeful American accent.

'Brilliant, isn't it,' I whispered back.

For the benefit of any non-golfers who might be reading this book – all three of you – I should explain why we were all so thrilled. Although the Belfry golf course isn't anything special (indeed, some have called it a waste of a decent pasture) it does have two exceptional holes: the eighteenth – a long par four with water down the left side and in front of the green that requires an accurate drive followed by an even more accurate long-iron shot, and the tenth. The tenth is a 320-yard par four across a stream to a green partially hidden behind trees. Of the two, the tenth is probably the best, especially in the context of a matchplay format like the Ryder Cup, where it comes at a pivotal stage of any match. It offers players a choice: they can either lay up short and chip on to the tiny green, or they can take a chance and attempt to drive the green. Golf course architects would call it a risk-reward hole. High handicap golfers would call it torture. However you describe it, the tenth was undeniably the best spot on the course from which to view the drama about to unfold. Anyone who had – as we did – a spot inside the ropes of this particular theatre could count themselves lucky.

But not quite yet. First, we had to undergo a crash course in the basics of marshalling delivered by Peter, a quietly spoken Brummie who introduced himself as our team leader.

My attention started to drift away from his voice after a couple of minutes. From what I did manage to learn, the basics of marshalling were basic indeed. Mostly, the job involved staying out of the way of the players. We were supposed to keep the crowd under control, although this depended largely on the goodwill of the crowd. Our one concrete power involved mobile phones and cameras. If we caught anyone using either we were to confiscate them (the items, not the users, smartarse), put them in a plastic bag and leave them at the left luggage tent where they could be retrieved at the end of play. Again, there was no explanation of how we could enforce this power. I improvised my own guideline: I would only confiscate items from people who were smaller and less aggressive than me.

In the event of anything dramatic – a riot, a fist-fight between the players or, as someone volunteered when asked to speculate on what might go wrong, a collapsing grandstand – we were to do absolutely nothing except call for help (though not in the middle of Tiger Woods's backswing). Big jobs were strictly the remit of those who had either more words on their armband, or a police badge and a gun.

Frankly, I was glad. My new American friend Steve, a lawyer from Seattle, was delirious. Less work meant more time to watch golf, which was the purpose of being a marshal in the first place. Peter seemed blissfully unaware of this truism. 'And I don't want to see anyone facing in and watching the golf. Our job is to watch the crowd,' he said, bringing his talk to an end.

Steve and I started laughing at that one. Which is where I believe my troubles began.

We then went for a walk down the fairway. Peter explained that our group had the responsibility of looking after the tenth hole and the eleventh hole, though not the eleventh green. That task belonged to the next group of marshals.

Each hole was split into three sections, and each section would be looked after by a subsection of our group. As we walked, he assigned people to their subsection. The good news was, I wasn't picked to look after the fairway crossing on the tenth. The only thing you could see from there was the corporate hospitality suites and I had no desire to spend three days watching computer software salesmen in white shirts eating canapés. The bad news was I wasn't picked to look after the tee or the green, or indeed anywhere on the tenth hole.

This little personal tragedy became apparent as we walked towards the eleventh tee. There were only eight of us left.

No one, not even a golf fanatic like me, had ever heard of the eleventh hole at the Belfry. I knew it existed, naturally, because all eighteen-hole golf courses have an eleventh hole, but what did it look like, what exciting moments in world golf had taken place there? I had no idea.

There was good reason for this anonymity. The eleventh was a featureless strip of mown grass at the outer edge of the course with nothing to offer except a view of a road and some rapeseed fields beyond.

'You.' Peter pointed at me. 'You can go up there, up the left-hand side of the fairway and do some ball spotting.'

About 250 yards out from the tee, the hole dog-legged to the right, beyond some trees which, in turn, obscured the view back towards the tee. There was a group of bunkers at driving distance. That was to be my station. There was no debate, no court of appeal. I had been appointed mayor of Nowhere, Golfsville. Steve was banished to the other side of the fairway crossing.

Violence doesn't come naturally to me but I was immediately overcome with a pulsing desire to grab our beloved team leader by the throat and choke the life out of him. But he was bigger than me, and he had more words on his armband.

I knew we shouldn't have laughed at the idea that we would spend the next few days watching the crowd and not the golf. This was his response. Let's see you get all excited at the sight of Ford Fiestas driving along a country road and fields of yellow buds swaying in the unseasonably warm winds of central England, he was saying.

'I don't want to go there,' I whined. 'There's nothing there to see.'

'We're not here to see, we're here to marshal,' he replied. 'In any case, you won't be staying there for the entire Ryder Cup. Everybody gets to move around. Just be patient. You'll get somewhere good.'

Somewhere good like crowd control at the toilet station in the tented village, no doubt.

Word filtered through that the first group of players was on the third hole and that it included Tiger Woods. This meant I had a couple of hours to chat to the people lining the fairway down by my vantage point, which I would gladly have done if there had been any people there. It was just me, a few trees and a bunker. Actually, I'm being unfair. There was a momentary burst of excitement when Peter Oosterhuis, the amiable and very tall former professional golfer, strode down the fairway, paced out the distance between my bunker and a bunker across the other side of the fairway (seventeen steps!!!!), then strode off towards the green, leaving me alone once again. The only detail missing from this landscape of deflated expectations was tumbleweed.

Who would ever have imagined the world's most exciting sporting event could be this mind-numbing, even in its preliminary, non-competitive stage? Not me, for one, and not you either, I suspect, which is why I decided to keep a detailed note of the morning's proceedings, an *aide-mémoire*. As evidence. It would come in handy if ever there was a court case (and believe me I was seriously considering suing the European Ryder Cup Committee for a breach of the Fair Treatment of Employees Act).

Time spent waiting for the marshalling to begin: Two hours.

Time spent marshalling: Depends on how you describe marshalling.

Go on: I spotted a ball.

A ball? One ball. It belonged to Niclas

Fasth. When I say I spotted it, he actually found it before I had the chance to tell him exactly where I had spotted it.

Did you see Tiger? Yes.

How did he look? Pissed off, and who can blame him. It must be difficult having a God-given talent, $200 million in the bank and a girlfriend who is so beautiful that other mortals – i.e. me – should feel themselves privileged to breathe the same air.

Tiger's girlfriend was in the gallery beside your bunker? No, no, I'm extemporising. I saw her picture in the morning paper.

Were there any people in the gallery when the practice matches passed through? Forty.

Any of them rowdy? Does eating an apple with your mouth open count as rowdy?

Not really: Then the answer is no.

How long did the golf action last? In total? Ten minutes.

Number of golf shots seen during that time: Around thirty.

Best shot: Lee Westwood's. An eight-iron to within five feet of the pin. Good club selection. Looks like he made the right choice of caddy.

Worst shot: Phillip Price. A six-yard pitching wedge from the rough into my bunker. Take my word for it, the man will be a liability to the European team once the tournament starts.

Number of friends caddying in the Ryder Cup: Six, including the great Andy Prodger. 'Bloody hell, it's you,' he said when he spotted me. 'They must be desperate if they're giving you a job.'

Number of friends who can't resist the chance to kick a man when he's down: One.

Overall, how was your first day? How many times do I have to say this? It was crap, rubbish, a waste of time, boring, tedious, I wished I'd stayed at home. This was not what I had been expecting. I was deeply, deeply disappointed.

When you say deeply disappointed, how deep is 'deeply'? Deeper than the deepest part of the deepest ocean. And then keep drilling. Don't stop until you get to the basement of the Starbucks on Kalawoonga Avenue, downtown Hobart, Tasmania.

There were six groups of four players. Once they had played through the eleventh hole, our job was finished for the day. Some of the other marshals from our section rushed off excitedly in the direction of the last few holes, hoping to watch some golf. I might have joined them but then my American friend Steve explained that even though we were marshals we did not have any special viewing privileges. There were some armbands that allowed inside-the-ropes access to virtually anywhere on the golf course but our orange armbands were good only for our particular section of the course. Once we stopped working, we had to take them off. In effect we were no better off than an ordinary member of the paying public.

'The only difference between them and us is that we've got to wear these terrible clothes,' Steve said, fingering the tank top he had not yet got round to throwing away.

My mind was made up. I decided not to hang around. There was the rest of the week in which to enjoy watching golf. I had other more pressing things to do, like buy a pair of black trousers, find a place to stay, and try to arrange a transfer from the eleventh fairway ball-spotting gulag.

I decided to tackle this list in reverse order.

I walked back to the marshals' headquarters in the hope of finding Barry and persuading him to move me somewhere else.

He was in a meeting. Of course he was. To pass the time until he was free, I wandered over to the driving range. Some players had already finished their practice round and were hitting balls, among them Padraig Harrington, who was taking swings with a towel tucked underneath his upper arms – very strange behaviour indeed, especially with the range of antiperspirant deodorants now available to the modern man.

The Irishman is one of my favourite golfers. There is the air of an innocent abroad about him. Even though he is a superb player, he has this wonderful expression on his face when he hits a great shot, like a wino who's just found a tenner in a jacket pocket. I watched him hit balls for a while and in the simple rhythm of his swing, the skill he showed in hitting six successive 120-yard wedge shots to within a few feet of each other, not to mention the pleasure he took from doing so, I remembered exactly why I love golf; exactly why I had made such an effort to get into the Ryder Cup. Padraig Harrington had made it to the Belfry and couldn't believe his luck. I had made it and couldn't stop whining. What an ungrateful bastard I had been since I'd got here, I thought to myself, and what a grateful bastard I intended to be from now on. With one condition – that I didn't have to spend the rest of the week spotting balls on the eleventh fairway.

I caught up with Barry just as he was climbing into a golf buggy.

'How are you doing? Have you got enough stuff for your magazine article?' he said.

Only if it was sixty words long.

'Oh, it's too early to say,' I said in the most self-pitying tone I could summon up. 'Actually, that's what I wanted to talk to you about.'

He pulled up. 'What's wrong?'

'Nothing. Well. It's just. It's just I'm a little worried about the article.'

I felt terrible lying like this, he seemed like such a decent man. 'The thing is, I'm stuck out on the eleventh hole. I thought I was going to be on the tenth, and that would have been great. But being out on the eleventh fairway spotting balls . . .'

'It wouldn't make for a very good article?'

'You could say that.'

'Do you want something a bit more in the thick of things?'

Exactly. 'Oh no, I don't want to put you to any trouble.'

He sighed, and I couldn't blame him. Eight hundred marshals under his charge, one huge golf tournament to keep under control and here he was wasting precious time on a solitary malcontent. A lying malcontent. He hesitated, looked at me. I smiled back, pitiably, like a wallflower in a borrowed dress trying to rustle up a dance.

'Hang on a minute,' he said, and dis-appeared back into one of the Portakabins. He re-emerged twenty seconds later and handed me a white armband.

'Take that,' he said.

'What is it?'

'A senior marshal armband. It'll give you access to just about anywhere on the golf course.'

I felt like Sally Field accepting her Oscar. You really love me, my brain said, though I managed to edit the thought before it reached my vocal cords. 'Thanks. That's very good of you.'

He climbed back into his golf buggy. 'Don't mention it,' he said, driving away. 'See you at the opening ceremony tomorrow.'

From ordinary marshal to senior marshal

in one day. A battlefield promotion. This was better than I could ever have hoped. I made a vow, silently of course, otherwise I would have been found out and then escorted to the nearest police van by a couple of my erstwhile colleagues. I *would* write a magazine article. Then I looked at my white armband, slipped it over my sleeve and gazed at it for a couple of minutes. Fuck it. Never mind a magazine article, I'd write a book. I'd call it *Confessions of a Senior Marshal* and I'd dedicate it to the Ryder Cup marshals. Most of all I'd dedicate it to Barry, without whom I would have been sitting at home.

One caveat. *Confessions of a Senior Marshal* would have to do without an eye-witness account of the opening ceremony. I've been a sports fanatic all of my life. I've even had the good fortune to attend some great events: the Olympics, the World Cup, the baseball World Series. All have left me with a psychotic aversion to opening ceremonies. They have nothing to do with sport and everything to do with making members of organising committees and CEOs of the corporate sponsors feel very self-important indeed.

I'd seen the Ryder Cup opening ceremony on television a few times. It wasn't as long or as bad as the others, not least because the wives of the American team usually turned up looking like off-duty lap dancers. With my new status as senior marshal, I'd probably be able to find a vantage point offering maximum titillation. Even so, I had no intention of going. The Ryder Cup would have its opening ceremony without me. I had better things to do, like find a hotel room within a fifty-mile radius of Birmingham city centre which cost less than Robert Downey Jnr's annual pharmacy bill.

Day One

THERE ARE PEOPLE WHO DEVOTE A GREAT deal of time to trying to stop the spread of golf courses. I know these people have a valid point. I'm aware, for instance, that the chemicals used to keep the greens looking pristine could seep into the water table and poison us all. I also know there are some golf courses, like the one I drove past last year in Death Valley, California, where using water to keep the fairways lush is a criminal use of a precious natural resource. There ought to be a law against this kind of environmental vandalism. I know this intellectually yet whenever I see a golf course I'm overcome by a feeling that is infinitely more powerful than intellect. I fall in love.

I drive by a golf course for the first time and it might be the ugliest golf course in the world, with tees the colour of baked mud and molehills on the greens, and I think to myself, 'God, you look gorgeous.' My heart speeds up. I take a second look and I begin to picture the long summer afternoons we could spend together, the triumphs we might share (but never, of course, the quadruple-bogey tragedies), and before I know what has happened I'm standing in the pro shop with my golf shoes on, bag at my feet, wallet open: 'One green fee, please.'

I admit I'm fickle. My feelings for certain golf courses have lasted no longer than a couple of bad shots. And I'm promiscuous. Ask me today the name of the greatest golf course in the world and the answer will be different from last week and will be different again next week. So understand me when I say that for a short time before play began on the first day of the 2002 Ryder Cup, I was absolutely, positively, head-over-heels in love with the Belfry.

It was an illusion, a fleeting romance, inspired partly by the moment – it was day one of the Ryder Cup and I was there! – and partly by the three years the course had just spent in the agronomist's beauty parlour. Like a bride on her wedding morning, she would never look more pristine and virginal.

The first match wasn't due to tee off for another hour and a half. I sat for a while in the empty grandstand behind the eighteenth green, imagining the shots I would play across water and the birdie putts I would hole, until I couldn't stand any longer the agony of not being allowed to walk into the pro shop, slap down my money and start hacking. I headed over to the marshals' HQ.

Already, hundreds of marshals were milling around. I was pleased to note that at least I now looked the part. I'd spent the previous day in Birmingham, trying to find a hotel room that cost less than £200 a night. When that particular project ended in abject failure I went shopping for a pair of black trousers to complete my marshalling uniform.

'You look very smart,' said Steve, my American friend.

'Thanks,' I replied, delving into my pocket to find my senior marshal's armband. 'And look.'

'Wow. Promotion. What did you do to earn it? Take a bullet for Monty?'

'I whinged to the chief marshal about being stuck out on the eleventh hole.'

'Ah yes,' he sighed. 'The place we Americans call Purgatory.'

'Don't tell me you're still out there spotting balls?'

'Oh no, I've been promoted to player transference from the tenth green to the eleventh tee,' he said, looking at his watch. 'In fact, I'm supposed to be out there right now for a meeting with the team leader.'

'Best of luck. Will you see any golf?'

'Absolutely fuck all,' he said, sadly. 'You?'

I didn't have the heart to tell him that as senior marshal without portfolio I was now free to wander wherever I wanted. Instead I told him about my efforts to find a place to stay for the duration of the cup, efforts which had led me to a motel somewhere in the east Midlands.

'The east Midlands?' Steve said.

'The place we Brits call Purgatory,' I replied.

I filled in a few details about my resting place – the broken shower, the chisel-faced hookers in the bar, the mouse droppings in the breakfast fruit salad, the £120 bill. This appeared to cheer him up no end and he wandered off to his meeting in a far happier mood. I stayed behind because I wanted to at least give the impression I was carrying out some research for my 'magazine article' about Ryder Cup marshals. Specifically, I wanted to know what possessed people to give up a week of their life to do what appeared to be a crushingly menial job for which they were paid nothing save an armful of ropey golf clobber. Was the world really full of fanatics who, like me, would do virtually anything if it meant getting a good view of the world's greatest golf tournament?

'Yes.'

'Yes.'

'Now that you mention it, yes.'

'Of course.'

'Actually, I just wanted to do my bit to make sure the tournament was a big success.'

Enough. Five marshals out of eight hundred isn't exactly a Gallup survey but I was getting bored. In any case, my half-hearted polling had already touched on something of the truth. Most of the marshals laughingly admitted they were only there for the golf but there were a handful who in the grand British tradition of *Dad's Army* seemed to think the event, possibly even the Empire, would stand or fall by their actions over the next three days. God knows where they got this idea. I've been at countless sporting events, music concerts and public gatherings and not once have I obeyed an instruction from a marshal unless he or she was built like an Olympic weightlifter. I looked around me. We were built like off-duty estate agents, office managers on a week's unpaid holiday and former *Guardian* journalists – all spindly legs, tidy hair and wire-rimmed spectacles. Even the official marshals' handbook acknowledged our collective wimpishness. 'If in doubt – stand still and do nothing,' it instructed on page two.

I, for one, was quite happy to stand still and do nothing. So, I suspect, was Denis, a zone captain whose job it was to fill me in on what a zone captain did. 'It'll help with your article,' Barry the chief marshal said, introducing the two of us.

Denis shook my hand. Grey-haired and placid, he smiled weakly from underneath his straw hat.

'So what d'you do?' I said, raking around in the bottom of my backpack for a pen and a notebook.

'Not much,' he said with a sigh. 'This and that. Make sure everything is OK in my little section.'

I wrote this down in my notebook. We walked out towards the third hole, with me pretending to take notes while Denis tried to summon up the energy to have a conversation this early in the morning. If I really wanted to know, he had recently retired from one of the big car companies, where he'd been a production line manager. The main reason he was here was to watch golf, naturally. In fact, since retiring he'd become something of a professional unpaid golf marshal. There was a group of friends who followed the European Tour around. 'It's a chance to meet up, watch a bit of golf, collect the free stuff.'

I nodded solemnly. 'Like a social club with waterproof tops?'

'Yeah. Right,' he said, ignoring my feeble efforts to brighten up his morning.

If the Ryder Cup marshalling army was really *Dad's Army*, and I'd decided that it was, then Denis was John Le Mesurier, the existentialist sergeant who was always keen to make a contribution to the greater good but struggled to find any real meaning to a marshal's life.

'And you like doing this? I mean, you don't seem exactly thrilled to be here,' I said.

'As long as nothing much happens, it's fine.'

We arrived at the third tee. Denis looked down the length of the fairway and I swear I saw him almost smile. The grandstands were not on fire, the fairways were mercifully free of rioting spectators. Nothing much was happening. We walked the length of the third fairway and then back down towards the fourth green. Denis spotted a fairway rope that needed tightening and wandered off, leaving me to guard a bridge between the fourth green and the fifth tee which was supposed to be used only by the players and their caddies. Who knows, one day there could be a plaque by this very spot: here on 27 September 2002, Lawrence Donegan performed his first duties as a golf tournament marshal.

'Can I go down there?' a spectator asked me.

'Eh, I don't think so.'

'Yeah, but can I?'

I looked around. No one was watching.

'Don't see why not.'

'Cheers, mate.'

Historians of marshalling may judge me harshly but at the time I didn't see the problem: the guy was in a hurry to meet his friends, there was no one on the golf course. It was a golf tournament, for Christ's sake, not East Berlin, 1968, and I was a marshal, not a Soviet rifleman guarding the wall.

I watched my co-conspirator walk over the bridge and out towards the fifth tee. Denis momentarily stopped trying to push a fallen fairway stake back into the ground to have a chat with the trespasser, who spread his arms in protest before pointing back at me. Traitor. Denis wasn't the type to give anyone a lecture but he seemed ready to give me a censorious look. Luckily, at precisely the moment our eyes met, a low, manly cheer rumbled across the golf course like a dropped bowling ball. I looked at my watch. It was 7.56. The first group of the 2002 Ryder Cup had stepped on to the first tee.

*

I already had my spot picked out. Behind the third tee was perfect. It was elevated, giving an uninterrupted view of the second fairway and green as well an oh-my-God-I-could-reach-out-and-steal-his-putter-while-he's-not-looking view of the players teeing off on the third. A couple of other marshals had had similar thoughts but when I got there, my white plastic senior marshal's armband pulled high up on my sleeve, they parted respectfully and let me stand between them.

Watching golf live without actually seeing any of the action is not something I'd recommend as a long-term activity but there is a visceral thrill to be had trying to work out what is happening using only one's patriotic prejudice and the noise of the crowd as a guide. For one thing, you can always make up any score you want to and the illusion will survive until reality makes its inevitable appearance.

The first match off was between Tiger Woods and Paul Azinger for the US, and Darren Clarke and Thomas Bjorn for Europe.

Judging by the distant but rousing cheers it was clear to the three of us that the Americans had conceded the match after one hole and were already back in the clubhouse being consoled by their wives. You can imagine our surprise when the thread of spectators along the second fairway began to thicken until it was twenty deep. This mass of humanity was soon followed by the players.

I saw Tiger first, walking down the centre of the fairway, wearing a blue tank top, grey trousers and a face like an undertaker's assistant. He'd bogeyed the first hole after hitting his second shot into a bunker, apparently because one of the photographers took a picture at the top of his backswing. Poor lamb was pissed off. Am I alone in thinking that even the greatest professional golfers are too quick to complain about 'distractions' on the course, especially when they make silly mistakes? After all, David Beckham still manages to take pretty decent free kicks while 40,000 opposition supporters are chanting that his wife takes it up the arse.

Azinger was next into view, wandering into the trees on the right side of the fairway. Bjorn looked white and drawn, like a man leaving the dock with a life sentence. Darren Clarke was last, lumbering, red-faced and smoking, the picture of ill health. A kid was carrying a board which read EUROPE 1UP. He had this dazed smile across his face, as if he'd just woken up inside his own perfect dream.

Me too. I found myself standing on my tiptoes, even though I had a perfect view. My fists were balled, even though I wasn't about to fight anyone. It was as if Clarke had just suffered a heart attack and Sam Torrance had asked me to come down and play the Irishman's second shot in to the green.

Just as well I didn't because I would have shanked it. Tiger, meanwhile, hit a sand wedge to eighteen inches.

He got a decent cheer from the home crowd but Clarke's shot, which landed ten times further from the hole, was greeted with ten times the noise. Azinger chopped his out into the bunker at the front of the green. Bjorn hit his as close as Clarke's and rolled in the putt, matching Woods's birdie.

Europe was still 1UP. Even more thrillingly, all four players were walking towards the third tee. I stood up tall, smoothed down my clothes and flattened my hair. Some people smoke cigarettes when they're nervous; I start obsessing about my appearance. I'm happy to dress like a tramp all day, every day, but stick me in a stressful place, a spiralling plane with its engines on fire, say, and I'll start cursing the fact that I didn't get a haircut before I left for the airport. I was this close to the greatest players in the game yet all I was thinking about were the crinkles in my waterproof top.

The players arrived on the tee and stood right in front of me. Tiger Woods – *Tiger Woods* – was less than two feet away, breathing the same air, surveying the same scene. Ken Comboy, whom I knew from my days as a bag carrier on the European Tour, was caddying for Bjorn. 'All right, Ken?' I mouthed, showing off to the other marshals that I knew people in all the right places.

'What the fuck are you doing here?' he replied with admirable frivolity, given the circumstances.

I would have kept the conversation up had we not been so rudely interrupted by Bjorn. 'Driver,' he snapped.

Ken handed him the club and stood back. He winked at me. Bjorn's shot went way right. Clarke was next up and with a wheezing swing sent his drive down the centre.

'Good shot,' Azinger said, tersely.

In the five or so minutes the four players were on the tee, these were the only words exchanged. Not even team-mates spoke to each other, preferring to stare at the ground or fiddle with their shirt sleeves. It felt as if I had just walked into the aftermath of some terrible family argument. I knew the Ryder Cup was life or death, but I didn't think it was this serious.

Azinger hit his drive, then his partner was

up. Like everyone else on the planet, I'd watched Woods on TV and marvelled at his brilliant golf but one of the failures of the cathode tube is its inability to accurately capture stage presence. Oddly, he seemed physically smaller in the flesh than I'd imagined, with long, piano player's fingers and a smooth, almost feminine face. He fixed his gaze on the ground, as if he was trying his best not to be noticed. I was almost fooled into thinking he wasn't anything special until he swung at the ball. And then it all became clear. In a single, wickedly violent but brilliantly precise act, the biggest sports star in the world revealed himself.

I watched his ball fly away and felt privileged to have witnessed its journey. Tiger bent down and picked up his tee, not bothering to look, as if he was bored by his own talent. And then they were gone, trailing an entourage of journalists and excited marshals; four oceangoing liners leaving port followed by a flotilla of smaller craft.

Those of us left behind were finally able to

breathe out and dissect what we had just witnessed.

'Did you see Woods?'

'See him? I was this close,' I said, raising my two forefingers inches apart.

'Do you think he ever smiles?'

'Come on, have you *seen* his girlfriend? 'Course he bloody well smiles.'

'Azinger hit it so far right on the first hole, they had to move the crowd back thirty yards,' someone said and we all fell silent, each of us imagining what a thrill it would have been to be able to move a crowd around, to have played even such a small, tangential part in golfing history.

There wasn't much time to contemplate our bad luck. The next group was already in the middle of the second fairway. I could see Sergio Garcia through the trees on the other side of the fairway. Europe was up in this match as well, according to the scoreboard at the back of the second hole.

I sometimes have occasions, born I think of spending a lot of my childhood alone at my grandmother's, when I invent games to keep myself amused – don't speak for the next two hours and you'll see a naked woman before Sunday; hold your breath for forty-five seconds and you'll never have to go to mass again. That kind of thing. Adulthood arrived long ago but the habit is hard to break. Don't look at the scoreboards for the entire tournament, I'd told myself before the week started, and you'll have a better time. I thought looking at scoreboards would spoil the thrill of the Ryder Cup. It took me just twenty minutes to work out that it adds to the thrill, in the same way that listening to the pitch of crowd noise is an essential part of the experience.

In any case, I have no willpower. I couldn't have stopped myself looking at the scoreboards. But I drew the line at the portable Ryder Cup radios (tuned to the shot-by-shot Ryder Cup radio station) that many people had hanging round their necks. That was a dilution of the live experience too far. The point of being at the Belfry was to watch the drama unfold before my eyes, not listen to it in my ear.

By the time the last of the four matches had played through the third tee Europe was up in two matches, down in one and level in the other, and I had bought myself a radio. As I said, I have no willpower.

The morning's work was now over for the other marshals on the third tee. As the marshals' handbook – chapter one, point (10) – said: 'If you are not working take off your armband and join the gallery.' Fortunately, that rule was only for ordinary marshals. I walked back towards the clubhouse, inside the fairway ropes of course, pondering the tricky problem of where to watch the matches reach their climax.

'The eighteenth, you fool,' I hear siren voices yell, but that shows inexperience. I'd bet my signed first edition of *Fever Pitch* that 95 per cent of matches have finished long before the eighteenth hole. So the eighteenth was out. Holes four to nine were also out because – of course – the matches couldn't finish on those holes. I briefly considered the tenth but when I got there Peter, the team leader who had banished me to ball-spotting purgatory during the practice day, was standing around looking like a copper in search of trouble. No doubt he'd find something for me to do and it would involve standing at a spot where I couldn't see anything. In any case, none of the matches would finish on the tenth and I really wanted to see someone deliver the final blow.

I looked at the scoreboard. The matches were all still close, which ruled out holes eleven to fourteen. This left fifteen, sixteen and seventeen. I chose the sixteenth, for the simple reason that it was just a short walk from the tenth tee.

When I got there the zone captain, a big, jolly, rugby type with cropped hair, was standing by the green. He was wearing black trousers, white shirt, a military tie and a golf club captain's blazer which was too long in the sleeves.

His name was H, one of the other marshals said.

I walked over and introduced myself. 'You H?'

He had a wrestler's handshake. 'That's me,' he said, grinning.

'How's the preparation, H?'

'Terrible, actually, we're down a few people. Come to help out?'

'Sort of.'

'Great to have you,' he said, resting his huge hand on my shoulder, then winking. 'Why don't you go and pick a spot?'

I picked my spot, by the passageway to the seventeenth tee, from where I had an eye-level view of the elevated sixteenth green. The grandstands had been full for two hours, according to Lisa, an older marshal who'd had the good sense to bring a fold-away chair and a couple of magazines. 'They've just been sitting there all day applauding the score-board,' she said, looking up from her copy of *Women's Realm* then nodding up at the spectators. 'Can you believe that?'

She had a point, and not just because the two people sitting on their backsides eating sandwiches by the sixteenth green scoreboard weren't exactly earning anybody's applause. 'How silly do you have to be before you'll spend £80 to sit and watch a scoreboard changing?' she sighed, flicking the page in disgust.

It was half an hour before the Woods group finally arrived. Despite a promisingly bitchy start Lisa wasn't the talkative type so I passed the time trying and failing to get rid of the white noise on my Ryder Cup radio. I walked over to the seventeenth tee. Nothing doing, so I went back to the side of the sixteenth, sat on the grass and flicked through Lisa's *Women's Realm*, looking for something interesting to read. In the end I gave up and watched the crowd watching the scoreboard, which was marginally more gripping than the knitting page but only just.

At least the news from out on the course was good: Europe was up in three matches, and down in one. Garcia, who was playing with Lee Westwood against David Duval and Davis Love, was on the verge of winning on the fifteenth green. I would have rushed over there but it would have meant battling through the crowds now flowing in our direction – led by the world's greatest golfer (and, judging by his grim expression, the world's most aggrieved man).

I decided to stay put, not least because Tiger's girlfriend had just been driven up to the green on the back of a golf buggy. It was parked less than ten yards to my right, roughly the distance now separating my eyeballs from my eye sockets. Blonde, blue-eyed and stylish (even in a golf jumper), Elin Nordegren looked as if she'd stepped off the pages of Italian *Vogue*. Seriously. I'd seen pictures of transcendentally beautiful people for years but until now I'd never seen evidence that they actually existed in the flesh.

I'm utterly ashamed to admit I couldn't stop staring at her and missed Thomas Bjorn rolling in a five-foot putt for a birdie. The European pair were now two up with two to play. Tiger strode past without even the briefest glance at Elin, which said more than a thousand magazine articles about his legendary powers of concentration.

He and the others had barely gone when Garcia and Westwood came down the fairway on the back of a buggy, taking the cheers of the crowd after having won their game on the fifteenth. It was probably a bit too early to start acting as if Curtis Strange had just signed a treaty of surrender but it was hard not to be swept along in the collective joy. I cheered as loudly as everyone else. Even Lisa allowed a smile to flicker across her face.

The players' buggy was rounding the back of the green when the scoreboard announced Montgomerie and Langer had beaten Scott Hoch and Jim Furyk. Within the space of five minutes Europe had won two matches and I had failed to witness either victory. I now had a choice. I could wait at the sixteenth for the final – and let's be honest, least glamorous – match of the morning, between Padraig Harrington and Niclas Fasth, and Phil Mickelson and David Toms, or I could head towards the eighteenth green in the hope that Elin would be waiting there for her boyfriend's match to finish. I decided after three nanoseconds of thought that this was no choice at all, so I thanked Lisa for her hospitality, informed Big H I had some important business to attend to elsewhere on the course and joined thousands of pathetic men, young and old, who'd clearly had the same idea as me and were heading towards the final green. We were all new recruits to Elin's Army.

Day Two

IN THE WEEKS BEFORE THE BELFRY SO MUCH sanctimonious rubbish had been written about bad crowd behaviour at the Ryder Cup, and about how the very future of the tournament was at risk, that one very important fact had been forgotten, which was this: it's usually the players who start the trouble.

Before 1983 you couldn't pay people to turn up and watch the Ryder Cup, never mind spend any time worrying about them fighting. Meanwhile, the players did everything but throw punches at each other. A few days before the 2002 match started there was a piece in the *Guardian* recounting the 1969 fourball match between Bernard Gallacher and Brian Huggett for the British team and

Ken Still and Dave Hill for the Americans, which started with an argument on the first green and went downhill from there. 'We didn't quite come to blows but it was as near to it as you could get without coming to blows,' Huggett said.

In 1957, American pro Tommy 'Lightning' Bolt broke his putter over his knee during a match against Scotsman Eric Brown. Truth be told, he really wanted to break it over Brown's head after an argument about gamesmanship.

For every club snapped, there had been fifty smaller, niggling disputes about the rules or whose turn it was to putt. When the teams weren't squabbling on the course, they were squabbling off it about clubs with illegal grooves, or not turning up at meetings to exchange team sheets. Most recently, there had been diplomatic incidents over Seve's terrible coughing fits and, of course, the American team's dance across the seventeenth green at Brookline. The nadir was Corey Pavin turning up to play wearing a

Desert Storm skip cap at Kiawah Island in 1991, which proved two things: there are some sportsmen who should never be allowed to watch television news without adult supervision and, secondly, Corey Pavin is a 24-carat numskull.

I'm not denying that Ryder Cup crowds have occasionally been out of order. When fans, such as those at Brookline in 1999, call Colin Montgomerie a fat, spoiled, red-haired baby there is nothing to say in their defence, except that three out of four isn't a bad effort. But more often than not those outside the ropes have taken their cue from those inside – as happened in 1969, when the police were called to make sure the Huggett/Gallacher match didn't end with the two American players being lynched. Likewise, when the police were called out to Southport and Ainsdale Golf Club to restore order to the 1933 Ryder Cup, it wasn't because of crowd riots, it was because the marshals (armed with long bamboo lances, according to Dale Concannon's terrific little book *The Ryder*

Cup: Seven Decades of Golfing Glory, Drama and Controversy) were unable to control the thousands of people who had crowded around Edward, Prince of Wales – all of them desperate to ask what he saw in an American divorcee with a face like a coal shovel.

When players are fist-pumping and high-fiving, it's only natural that the crowd gets a little boisterous. Big deal. Cheering missed putts by the visiting team is as much a Ryder Cup tradition as the players turning up to play in pink cashmere jumpers and wine-coloured trousers. Both are unacceptable in an ideal world but how can you legislate against either of them? This is sport, not the Bolshoi Ballet or London fashion week; players should be allowed to dress like off-duty gameshow hosts and fans should be allowed to behave like fans.

However, having said all of that, when I walked into the bar in the tented hospitality village after the first day's play had finished I thought I'd walked into Caligula's pantry. The place was ankle deep in beer. I had to duck to miss a flying pizza slice. Europe, everybody's underdogs including mine, were ahead four and a half points to three and a half and some fans had decided it was time to break out the champagne, or at the very least to guzzle the watery lager. A good time was being had by all, aided somewhat by a loud, tight jazz band fronted by the most sensational-looking blonde woman I'd seen since, well, since Tiger's girlfriend. She was belting out a great version of Van Morrison's 'Moondance' although her voice was somewhat outshone by her outfit – a knee-length, off-the-shoulder red dress which was tighter than sausage casing.

'What a marvellous night to make romance 'neath the moon and stars up above,' she sang.

'Get your tits out for the lads,' the group of leery, red-faced boors at the front of the small stage in the corner chanted back.

Not that I'm averse to women wearing skin-tight dresses (although I admit to finding leery, red-faced boors a bit tiresome) but this wasn't what I was after. I was after a peaceful corner of a peaceful bar, a quiet place where I could enjoy a pint and reflect on the day's events.

In one respect, the day's events were more accurately described as non-events. Walking from the golf course to the tented village, I had done a mental tally of my day's efforts as a marshal. For about an hour in the afternoon I had manned a rope across the access path between the sixteenth green and seventeenth tee – over which, incidentally, Scott Verplank had almost tripped. Notwithstanding the fact that if ever there was a golfer in the world who looks like he deserves to be tripped up it is Scott Verplank, this was hardly a significant contribution to the smooth running of the Ryder Cup.

The fact was, there was nothing for me to do. There was nothing much for any marshal to do, at least not that I could see. People were behaving themselves, for a variety of reasons – because the players were behaving themselves, because there was no alcohol allowed on the golf course, because Prince Charles wasn't there and therefore no one wanted to ask him what he saw in an English divorcee with a face like a coal shovel – but mostly, I guess, because they were too engrossed in the golf.

After all of the talk about crowd trouble, the predictably cringeworthy opening ceremony (which thankfully I'd managed to avoid) and the shock at seeing machine-gun-carrying cops wandering around the course, the sport of golf had almost been forgotten about. Not any more. 'I'll never have more fun than I did out there today,' Niclas Fasth said after the first day's play was over.

He wasn't the only one, although Tiger, who ended up losing twice, was reported by the US captain Curtis Strange to be 'not feeling too good'. He looked positively deathly the last time I saw him, standing by the edge of the green while Lee Westwood holed out to give the Europeans a point in the second of the afternoon foursomes.

At that stage it looked as if Europe would

finish the first day with at least a three-point lead. But the Americans staged something of a comeback, led by the unlikely pairing of Verplank and Hal Sutton, a man who many self-regarding, self-appointed experts in the world of golf – such as me – believed would be a complete liability to the American team. Nothing could have been further from the truth. 'I was out there with this old horse and I rode him like the wind,' Verplank said after he and his partner came back from two down with six holes to play to beat Bjorn and Clarke. After close textual analysis of Verplank's remarks, linguistics experts later said they believed they were intended as a compliment, although it should be noted that the two Americans didn't play together again over the weekend.

The Americans won a second point in the foursomes when Stewart Cink and Jim Furyk defeated Padraig Harrington and Paul McGinley, then sneaked another half-point as Colin Montgomerie and Bernhard Langer lost a two-up lead over the last four holes in their match against Mickelson and Toms. Langer had a chance to win on the eighteenth but couldn't even hit the hole with his putt. It's probably just as well, otherwise the bar in the tented village might have been even rowdier.

I left Miss Moondance facing her admirers with nothing to defend herself but a strong pair of lungs and a microphone stand and headed off into the night.

My plan was to spend every minute of day two on the tenth tee. Over a pint and fish and chips that night, I compared notes with Tom Jenkins, the *Guardian*'s ace photographer and the man whose photograph of me (dis)graces the cover of this book. I confess to feeling slightly envious. He'd spent part of the first day with his long lens at a spot just down the tenth fairway, taking shots of the players teeing off. 'It's the best sporting theatre I've ever experienced,' he said. 'You've got to get yourself down there.' Coming from Tom, who's been at every memorable sporting event of the last ten years, this was quite a recommendation. My mind was made up.

I turned up at the marshals' headquarters at quarter to seven the next morning, refreshed and ready to wheedle myself a decent seat at the theatre.

In the end, I didn't have to try too hard. 'Sure, if you like,' Barry the chief marshal said when I asked permission to spend the day on the tenth. 'In fact, I think they could do with some extra help over there. That's a very busy spot. Very exciting over there.' First Tom, now Barry. The only person left to convince was my former team leader Peter – and even he had to concede that a chief marshal's express instruction trumps a team leader's personal antipathy.

'As long as you don't get in people's way,' he said, wandering off towards the eighteenth green.

'No need to worry about that, Napoleon,' I replied, but not until he was out of earshot.

At least some of the other marshals were glad to see me. 'We've missed you,' yelled

Steve the American lawyer. ' Man, this is the best place to be on the golf course. The absolute best.'

'I thought you were supposed to be helping players walk from the tenth green to the eleventh tee,' I said, sourly.

'Fuck that, man,' he laughed. 'I applied for a transfer from transference yesterday lunchtime. What about you? Where have you been?'

'The sixteenth.' I explained that I'd seen some exciting things too: great iron shots, holed chips, long putts, David Toms's wife, Tiger's girlfriend. Why, I was right there yesterday when one marshal had tried to break Scott Verplank's neck.

Steve shook his head. 'No, man – it's nowhere near as good over there. Here, you get to see everything – and then when everything is finished here, you walk down to the eighteenth green and watch everything there.'

He pointed to a spot behind the tenth tee that looked directly down the line of the players' drives and on to the green. 'That, my friend,' he sighed, 'is golfing nirvana.'

The morning matches were just about to tee off. It would be a couple of hours before they reached us but nirvana had already been claimed by someone, a steely-face marshal I'd never seen before who was clasping a 'Quiet Please' sign to his chest as if it was a samurai sword. Nelson's Column has never looked more permanent than he did.

Even if I'd wanted to take his place, which I obviously did, I didn't get the chance. Peter came back from the eighteenth green, found a crowd of us loitering around the tenth tee and dispatched us to our posts. I was assigned to the group looking after the crossing halfway down the tenth fairway. We could see the players hit their second shots, though not what happened to the ball when it landed on the green. For that we had to rely on the response from the crowd and the people in the corporate hospitality suites. (As a general rule, if an American's ball landed anywhere near the hole, the crowd applauded politely and the people in the hospitality suites walked over to the free bar and poured themselves a large Scotch. If a European ball went close, the crowd roared and the people in the hospitality suites walked over to the free bar and poured themselves a large Scotch.)

Our job was to close off the fairway as soon as the players arrived on the tee and make sure no one trespassed until each match had played through. We would have succeeded had it not been for the general public. For a nation which has spent centuries on bended knee before a ludicrous shower of chancers called the Royal Family, the British have a surprisingly strong anti-authoritarian streak. Maybe it's because we're more impressed by gilded coaches than plastic armbands. Since when did 'Please don't walk over there just now, you could get hit on the head by Darren Clarke's golf ball' translate as 'Please walk across there and get hit on the head by a golf ball in front of 700 million television viewers worldwide'?

The morning matches started well for

Europe and were split two points apiece – a good result for Europe, especially as Torrance had virtually conceded a point in the first match, pairing up two of his – how can I put this? – 'less intimidating' players, Pierre Fulke and Phillip Price. Mind you, the pair were level standing on the tenth tee in their match against Mickelson and Toms.

Tiger Woods was in the last match of the morning, paired with Davis Love, against Clarke and Bjorn. The Americans were two up at the turn, though clearly this hadn't improved Tiger's mood.

'Come on guys, do your job!' he yelled at us from the front of the tee.

'Sorry, Tiger,' we whispered back as we tried to shoo away a couple of stragglers standing in the middle of the fairway who were looking back at the tee, wondering who the angry guy doing all the shouting was.

Once that group had gone through I walked over to the eighteenth green, where a huge television screen had been set up opposite the arc of the grandstand. The sun's glare made it hard to follow what was happening but I managed to see Price miss a putt on the seventeenth to give the match to the Americans. Tiger then holed a putt on the fifteenth to win his match, which put his team ahead overall for the first time. Fortunately, Garcia and Westwood held on for a win. Europe was back in the lead, by half a point. Only the Montgomerie and Langer against Verplank and Hoch match looked like it had a chance of coming down the final hole. I would have stayed to watch but there was business to attend to back on the tenth tee.

The steely-faced marshal behind the tenth tee was called Derek. It was one of God's cosmic jokes, as well as my good fortune, that he'd given Derek the physique of a nightclub bouncer and the nature of a nursery school teacher. 'Hi, Derek,' I said, pulling my senior marshal's armband out of my pocket and waving it in his face. I'd decided on a bold approach. 'Listen, you're going to have to move.'

I stole a glance down the wide, open fairway and I swear my legs began to shake. It was if my entire golfing life had been a long journey leading me to this square yard of mown grass in the Midlands. I'd been looking at the tenth hole for four days now but I'd never seen it like this: lush, inviting, beautiful, completely revealed – a Rubens painting if Rubens had painted golf holes instead of naked women.

'Sure,' Derek said, smiling.

'The thing is, the boss says we need a senior marshal on the job.'

'No problem.'

'Yeah, apparently there was some trouble on the fairway with some crappy marshals this morning and they want someone senior to keep an eye out.'

'Great. I can go and get my lunch.'

I wasn't listening to what he was saying. I never listen when I'm lying because I'm concentrating too hard on making sure my face doesn't turn the colour of an irradiated strawberry.

'Listen, there's no point in taking that attitude. If you've got any complaints speak to the boss,' I said, slightly hysterical now.

'Do you want this "Quiet Please" sign?' he said, looking puzzled.

Suddenly, my brain began to function again. 'Excuse me?'

'The sign – do you want it?'

My own 'Quiet Please' sign? Of course I wanted it. I'd wanted one since the moment I arrived. Being a marshal without a 'Quiet Please' sign was like being Batman without a cape; or Superman without a pair of blue tights; or Pamela Anderson without three bucketfuls of silicon bursting out of her bra. The signs seemed to be in short supply and I hadn't had the bare-faced cheek to ask Barry the chief marshal for one, especially as I'd already pushed my luck to its limit with the senior marshal armband. My best hope was that one of the other marshals would leave theirs lying around and I could nick it. Fat chance. The Belfry was full of pathetic losers like me who wanted a souvenir of what was turning out to be a sporting occasion for the ages.

Perhaps Derek could sense my desperation. Perhaps he'd already nabbed himself half a dozen signs and felt like making a desperate man happy. I didn't stop to ask.

He handed me the precious paddle. I held its polystyrene handle in my sweaty grip and and I swear I felt a surge of power up my arm, like Luke Skywalker wielding a lightsaber for the first time.

'Great, thanks.'

He stared straight into my eyes. 'I'm going now. Are you all right?' he said.

'No, no. I'm fine. I'm great, actually.'

The afternoon matches hadn't even started yet. I tried to make myself as inconspicuous as possible in case Peter saw me and decided my talents were needed elsewhere. As it turned out, I needn't have worried. My talents were exactly where they were needed, as evidenced by my only act of bona fide marshalling during the entire Ryder Cup: a heroic attempt to ensure the smooth transition of spectators between the tented village and the golf course which almost saw me crushed to death by a stampeding crowd.

The problem with stories about nearly being crushed to death by a stampeding crowd, as opposed to stories in which you actually *are* crushed to death by a stampeding crowd, is that they aren't anywhere near as exciting, so I'll keep this short.

There was a bottleneck behind the tenth tee – a narrow path that served both as a thoroughfare between the tented village and the course, and as a viewing point for people who want to stand and watch players talking to each other on the practice putting green. Why anyone would want to do such a thing, I have no idea. I've listened to professional golfers talking to each other on the practice putting green and, trust me, it's not Kierkegaard and Marx debating the existence of God. Nevertheless, more and more people gathered and rather than move on when asked, they stayed put, with the predictable outcome that no one could go anywhere.

A pushing match developed between those spectators who wanted to gawk at golfers talking to each other and those spectators who wanted to get to the course. Personally, I would have left the two camps to shove each other into exhaustion but then I have an underdeveloped sense of social responsibility. However, Peter the team leader could write books on social responsibility, which is why he appeared from nowhere to restore order. 'What are you doing standing there? Give me a hand!' he yelled at me, before disappearing into the crowd. Not wishing to alienate him further, I did what I was told, falling over a temporary crash barrier as I tried to get into the middle of the crush. This is how I almost came to be trampled underfoot.

I didn't die, obviously, though a tall, agitated man in a washed-out red windcheater called me a fucking Nazi, which was pretty hurtful. He wanted my name, rank and serial number. I deserved to be sacked for throwing my weight around, apparently. 'Lance Corporal Donegan, the boogie-woogie bugle boy of Company B, Her Majesty's Royal Marshalliers,' I replied, easing people along with an authority that surprised me.

It took us ten minutes to clear the pathway and, silly though it sounds, when our minuscule drama was over I felt a mountainous sense of achievement. I had contributed. When the history of the Cup came to be written I would be there; not in the official version, perhaps, but definitely playing a starring role in the golfing fable that would be handed down through generations of Donegans.

Peter seemed content too — content enough, in any case, to let me return to my treasured spot behind the tee. He watched me take my place, then shook his head and gave me an indulgent smile. 'Don't stand in the players' eye line,' he said. 'And remember — you're supposed to be watching the crowd, not watching the golf.'

'Sure thing, boss,' I replied, turning to face the three-deep line of people now gathered behind the crash barriers, waiting for the players to arrive. And there my attention remained for thirty seconds – long enough for Peter to disappear out of sight.

If I could remember what happened when three of the four afternoon matches passed through the tenth – every bead of sweat, every sigh, every word exchanged, every shot – I'd pass the details on. But I can't. I didn't have a notebook. In any case, I was too wrapped up in the moment to do anything as mundane (or as responsible) as take notes. I vaguely recall that Jesper Parnevik was playing with Niclas Fasth and that Parnevik hit his drive into the stream at the front of the green. Phil Mickelson looked fatter than I'd imagined, Colin Montgomerie thinner, and Scott Hoch more pissed-off than a millionaire sportsman had any right to be.

However, I do recall the fourth match – between Woods and Love for the Americans and Garcia and Westwood for the Europeans – as if it is tattooed on the inside of my eyelids. They were on the tee for just over four minutes. I've got every second on video – a present from a friend of mine who was watching the television broadcast on the other side of the world.

Garcia drove first, and with a wild swing sent the ball towards the trees at the front of the green. It ricocheted off a branch and landed on the front edge. Westwood then stepped on to the tee. The chanting began, quietly at first: *driver, driver, driver* . . . The two Europeans talked for what at the time seemed like an hour but was in fact – I've timed it – forty-eight seconds. Finally, Westwood reached into his golf bag and pulled out the driver. The crowd roared. The camera flashed over to Garcia – now standing to the left of the tee, from where he could see the green – then back to Westwood. And there I am, standing behind him. Zelig.

I look old and serious, like my grandfather trying to pick the winners from the Saturday morning racecard: lips pulled tight with concentration, eyes fearful, staring straight down the fairway when I should be facing the

crowd, my 'Quiet Please' sign raised high –
captured for ever in what the television
commentator on my tape described as 'one of
the most dramatic moments in the history of
golf'.

Behind me – and I'm ashamed to say I take
a perverse pleasure in this – several people are
craning their necks to look past me. I was
blocking their view of the action. To those
people: I'm sorry but, really, it's your own
fault. You should have volunteered to become
a marshal.

After the trophy had been presented the
following day I spoke to Westwood very
briefly. 'Best shot of all time,' I told him. 'It
were all right,' he replied, brushing off the
compliment as if it was a crumb on the front
of his shirt.

It's impossible to support golfers in the
way you support a football team like, say,
Celtic. For a start, golf doesn't encourage the
warm communal experience. There's no
social backdrop to the events taking place out
on the course and little shared history among

the spectators. You can't wear a Lee Westwood scarf, at least not unless you want to be locked up for stalking. Having said that, if wearing scarves at golf tournaments was suddenly made compulsory, I would always wear a Lee Westwood scarf. When I caddied in the same group as him in Germany, Westwood's father caddied for his son, pulling his bag along on a trolley. I thought that was touching. I also liked the fact that he remembered my name long after my caddying days were over and I was back to being a journalist, and he was making millions on the golf tour – vanity on my part, I guess. But it's the little things that matter in human relationships, isn't it? That's why I always made a point of following his career.

In the year leading up to the Ryder Cup, he'd had a terrible time. He'd fallen down the world ranking from number five to somewhere in the 140s. By all accounts, he couldn't hit a straight drive, or a decent iron shot, or hole any putts. Before the tournament started, serious golf writers were calling on him to stand down in favour of someone – anyone – who wouldn't be such an embarrassment. Westwood laughed it off but he must have felt the pressure all weekend. Never more than at that moment, standing on the tenth tee with thousands of spectators craning to catch sight of him, and with Tiger Woods watching – all of them waiting to see if he would live up to his recently acquired reputation of being a dud.

And yet despite all of this, he hit the best golf shot I have ever seen. That's why, for the first time in my life, I wanted to run on to the tee and hug a professional golfer the way I frequently want to run out on the Parkhead pitch and hug Henrik Larsson. 'The best shot in the history of golf,' I said. I meant it, too.

So.

So let me tell you that the best shot of all time looked like the long, lazy, white arc of a transatlantic jet. Westwood's drive soared 310 yards and moved twenty yards left in mid-flight. Twenty yards, precisely – enough to catch the left edge of the partially hidden green. Watching it I felt exhilarated, as if I was riding on the back of the ball, the wind pushing back the skin on my face until it was taut. I was amazed by the beauty of the view, the smoothness of the ride, the sweet science that carried me from there to here.

'Here' was a spot thirty feet from the pin.

When it landed on the green, Garcia leapt into Westwood's arms and the two of them danced to the noise of the crowd going berserk. Woods and Davis looked on disdainfully, like the two ugly sisters in a panto.

'Might as well go for it,' I thought I heard Love say, but then Woods reached into his bag, pulled out an iron and gave his ball a prosaic dunt down the middle of the fairway. Love followed suit, and the two Americans trotted off to jeers and the odd shout of 'Cowards'.

'A certain victory to Europe,' I remember thinking to myself. Which goes to show you how much I know about golf.

*

The US won the first of the afternoon fourballs, when Mark Calcavecchia and David Duval closed out Niclas Fasth and Jesper Parnevik on the last hole. Colin Montgomerie, who was becoming the star not just of the European team but of the entire event, guided Padraig Harrington to victory over Mickelson and Toms, while Darren Clarke and Paul McGinley managed to scrape a half against Hoch and Furyk. That left Garcia/Westwood versus Woods and Love to decide whether or not Europe would take a lead into the final day.

It wasn't quite anarchy by the side of the eighteenth green as the four players walked down the fairway, but the crowd on the inside of the crash barriers was almost as big and as boisterous as the crowd on the other side. Marshals, journalists, players, players' wives and caddies had all gathered under the tree to the right of the green to watch them finish. Word had gone out that it had been the best match of the tournament. 'The best match of all time,' I heard someone say (which made it the sixth 'best match of all time' since yesterday).

Perhaps not, but there was a scale to the choreography – the fading sun, the cloud-streaked, deep blue sky, the yellowy dust kicked up by the feet of a thousand rushing fans – that made it feel as if the four players were playing with the future of mankind at stake.

It all came down to Westwood, who had to hole a downhill four-footer to give Europe a half-point and the lead going into the final day. He missed. Of course he missed. No one with human feelings would have been able to hole the putt in such circumstances. In a way I was glad he missed; the tiny imperfection simply added to the perfection of the day. Only the singles matches remained and the two teams were now tied with eight points each.

As I said – perfection.

Final Day

IN A WELCOME REMINDER THAT EVEN professional golfers possess a spiritual side, players from the two teams requested that a church service be held before the start of the final day's proceedings. If only any of them had bothered to turn up the reminder would have been even more welcome. Not even Bernhard Langer, golf's most famous Christian, made it, which left the vicar and his choir to celebrate the service before a row of empty chairs laid out on the patch of rough between the ninth and eighteenth greens.

I don't know if the poor vicar was offended but everybody else who was there was offended on his behalf. I watched the service from the back of the green with a couple of journalist friends. We passed the time in between hymns discussing who was going to win the Cup. Traditionally the Americans had been the strongest team in the singles matches, but when the draw was announced the previous night it appeared that Curtis Strange had eaten a magic mushroom omelette before choosing his line-up. All of his best players – Woods, Mickelson, Love, Furyk – were playing in the closing matches, where they wouldn't be able to influence the final outcome if Europe managed to win enough of the earlier pairings. Sam Torrance, meanwhile, had done the exact opposite – putting his best players at the top of the line-up in the hope of building up an early lead then coasting to victory on the momentum generated by winning early points.

I thought briefly about nipping across to the on-course bookmakers but gambling straight after a church service seemed a bit too sacrilegious, even for an atheist like me. Instead, I walked across the course to the marshals' headquarters to look for Barry the chief marshal.

He'd probably be rushing around later in the day and I wouldn't be able to find him. I wanted to say thanks, and congratulations: thanks for welcoming me to the marshalling fraternity; thanks for my promotion to senior marshal; thanks for showing me that it is possible to carry out a responsible job without throwing your weight around like a five-star general; and congratulations on presiding over a tournament which hadn't had a single instance of trouble.

'You must be very proud,' I told him.

'There's time yet,' he sighed.

'You sound disappointed. Were you hoping for a riot?'

This wasn't as far-fetched as it might seem. I'd spoken to some marshals who were crushed that they hadn't had any miscreants to wrestle to the ground or escort to the exit.

'Definitely not,' he said. ' Mind you, I won't be able to sit down until the final putt has been holed. What about you? Where are you going to watch today?'

'I thought I'd start at the first hole. I've never actually seen any of the matches start and I thought it would be good to watch professional golfers try to swing a golf club while paralysed with nerves.'

'Good choice,' he said.

We sat and talked for a little while longer about crowd behaviour, golf tournaments in general and the Ryder Cup in particular. The delay caused by the terrorist attacks in America meant he'd been planning for this year's tournament since 1998. He was a volunteer. He'd been paid nothing. But get this: he would have paid money to do the job.

The only disappointment was that he'd hardly seen any live golf.

'Me neither,' I said, laughing. 'Only about six hours a day.'

'I've seen a few shots on the big screens but other than that I think I've seen about two shots actually being hit. Maybe I'll get a chance today,' he said, getting up from his seat. He had another meeting to attend somewhere on the golf course. A chief marshal's work is never done. My work, on the other hand, never starts so I wandered over to the practice ground and watched the players hit balls for a while.

This is not a sentence I'd ever thought I'd type, but Colin Montgomerie provided the main entertainment of the morning. Something had happened to the Scot during the course of the 2002 Ryder Cup, something strange. Usually, he walks around a golf course like a man under the impression that smiling gives you herpes but for the last few days he'd been laughing, making jokes, mucking around with the fans. Presumably, all of this had something to do with the fact he'd played brilliantly all week.

I'd followed Montgomerie's mercurial moods closely enough down the years to know this wasn't a permanent transformation, but it was welcome while it lasted. And entertaining. Today's pre-game performance revolved around a fan who heckled him after he'd hit a bad shot on the range. 'Come on out here and see if you can do better,' Montgomerie shouted back.

The fan came out and hit a few shots while the tournament comedian stood with his hands on his hips and laughed at his pathetic efforts. Perhaps you had to be there, but, trust me, the performance was funny and touching and a perfectly light-hearted start to what promised to be a seriously tense day. When it finished I headed out towards the course with a smile on my face.

I bumped into D.J. Russell on the way. A former golf pro, all-round good guy and member of Sam Torrance's back-up team, D.J. had been on the European Tour when I first met him. Back then, he was always good for a bit of locker room gossip so, naturally, I asked him to fill me in on the backstage bickering between the players, the drunken shenanigans, the wife-swapping, the illicit bugging of the American team room in order to find out Curtis Strange's tactics.

Either none of this had actually happened

or D.J. had become very discreet in his old age. All he would tell me was this: 'We couldn't believe it when we saw the draw. If we can't win now we'll never win.'

The galleries around the first tee were twenty deep. After row three it was impossible to see anything other than the back of people's heads. A few lucky spectators had bagged spots at the back of the grandstand behind the eighteenth green, from where they had a perfect view of the opening shots. I walked through the crush, flashed my armband and took a spot on the little grassy bank just inside the spectator barriers, taking special care not to block anyone's view. (Come on, I'm brazen but not that brazen.)

Match one was due off at quarter past eleven. At 11.05, Colin Montgomerie and Sam Torrance strode purposefully down the steps leading from the practice putting green to the tee. Torrance had his hand on his player's shoulder. He was wearing the kind of smile fathers reserve for the day they escort their daughter down the aisle. The happy couple were followed a couple of minutes later by a grim Curtis Strange and a morose Scott Hoch.

Hoch has a reputation as a world-class whiner, so his hunched shoulders and sour expression came as no surprise. Less well known is that Montgomerie has never been Hoch's greatest fan. It started back at the 1997 Ryder Cup, when the two played each other in what turned out to be a poisonous singles match. Back then Montgomerie had been denied a win because Seve Ballesteros, elated that the Cup had been secured, conceded a thirty-foot putt to the American. Maybe I was reading too much into a simple handshake but from where I was standing it looked like the two players wanted to wrestle rather than play eighteen holes.

Photographs were taken, announcements made, last-minute instructions whispered in the ear. 'If he's got a putt to win the match, attack him with the three-wood,' I imagined Sam Torrance telling his man.

'On the tee ... Colin Montgomerie,' declared Ivor Robson, the suave, silver-haired starter.

It's long been my view that truly great golf shots should be judged on context. For instance, I have actually had a hole in one. Was it a great golf shot? Of course not. I was playing on my own on a wet Tuesday in Donegal and I was 26 over par at the time. No one was there to see it, apart from me. Indeed, as the years have passed the more I have begun to think the entire episode might have been a dream.

By contrast, Colin Montgomerie's tee shot was a truly great golf shot. It was the first shot on the most important day of the greatest golf tournament in the world. He was surrounded by thousands of people. Millions of people were watching him on television. In the circumstances, I would have been expecting a round of applause if I'd demonstrated the ability to stand up straight. Montgomerie not only stood up straight, he hit a three-wood 300 yards down the left side of the fairway. If he'd rented a car, filled the tank full of rocket fuel and brought along an Ordnance Survey map of the west Midlands he couldn't have sent the ball any further or placed it in a better spot.

As soon as Montgomerie stepped to the side of the tee, taking extra care not to follow the flight of the ball, I knew it was a guaranteed point to Europe. I'm equally certain Scott Hoch knew this too, which is why he semi-duffed his tee shot about eighty yards short of his opponent's.

The next match, between Sergio Garcia and David Toms, had just teed off when there was a huge roar from the first green. Either Montgomerie had holed a birdie putt to go one up or Scott Hoch had fallen backwards into a bunker. The news floated back: Montgomerie had holed a putt.

Clearly, Curtis Strange had noticed Torrance's fatherly approach to escorting his players to the tee and injected a bit more warmth into his entrances. David Toms got the arm around the shoulder treatment from his captain. Hal Sutton did too, then David Duval. At one stage I thought Strange was about to give Mark Calcavecchia a French kiss to help him on his way. Torrance responded by ratcheting up the proud father quotient. Big smiles, warmer hugs, fonder goodbyes. By the time match eleven, between Phillip Price and Phil Mickelson, was due up on the tee, I was beginning to think I was at one of those Moonie ceremonies where hundreds of brides are led up the aisle to get married.

I once read somewhere that many of the people who participated in these mass religious ceremonies were there under duress; that they'd either been kidnapped or drugged by the church fanatics and forced to take part. Phillip Price looked like he'd been both kidnapped and drugged. I don't mean to be unkind to the Welshman, especially as I've hardly said anything positive about him thus far, but he looked utterly petrified as he waited to hit his first tee shot. By contrast, Mickelson looked around like Conan the Barbarian with a superiority complex.

While the first tee was a montage of Welsh terror and American swagger, cheers were rising from all other points of the course. The scoreboard over by the practice putting green was already turning blue – signifying that the European players were leading – and I was missing out on the action. I decided I didn't need to see all twelve matches start, that it would be more exciting to be out on the course. The question was, where?

Plan A was to follow the noise; a plan I later renamed the Stupid Plan. By the time I got to where the noise was, the caravan had moved on and another roar would roll in from somewhere else.

I looked at the scoreboard behind the fourth green. Montgomerie was up, Harrington was up, Garcia was up, Langer was up, Clarke was up. Europe was thrashing America and I had seen virtually no action of any significance. I started panicking. Rather than walking briskly around the course, I started sprinting. This improved matters, but not by much. I arrived at one green in time to see Montgomerie acknowledging the crowd's applause as he walked towards the next tee – heartening but hardly a Ryder Cup memory to impress strangers with on transatlantic flights.

More urgently, I was knackered. It was sunny, warm, and I was still wearing my marshal's windcheater. My shirt was sticking to my back, my armpits were beginning to smell tropical. It was time for Plan B.

Plan B was to give away my windcheater to the first person I met, untuck my shirt to let the fresh air do its work and then get over to the tenth tee – scene of my greatest marshalling triumph (and I'm not talking about my brief foray into the field of crowd control by the practice putting green). Why hadn't I thought of it before?

When I got there team leader Peter was prowling around. Now that *détente* had been established between us I thought it would be a simple matter of asking straight out if I could get my spot back. 'You'll be giving us marshals a bad name,' he said before I'd even opened my mouth.

'What do you mean?'

'Standing right behind the players like that. I saw you yesterday – right in their eye line.' He shook his head, which I took to mean that our relationship had entered yet another phase, one that involved me asking him if I could stand behind the tenth tee and him telling me to get lost, that Colin Montgomerie does the Ryder Cup comedy.

Of course, there were several points I could have made, not least that none of the players had complained about me or to me. But the fact was, he was absolutely right. I had broken one of the golden rules. 'Never stand on or near the swing line,' it said in the marshals' handbook. The sentence was even underlined, as I'm sure Peter would have pointed out had I made the mistake of defending my conduct.

I didn't want an argument. For one thing, the poor bloke had enough to contend with and could do without insubordination from the ranks. For another thing, there was a marshals' party after the close of play. I wasn't sure if Peter had any influence over the guest list but I didn't want to risk being locked out while wild celebrations were taking place on the other side of a plate glass door.

I took a deep breath and smiled. I shook his hand and thanked him for being such an inspiring leader. If ever I became chief marshal at a European PGA Tour event – which, as you've probably worked out by now, is not likely – I would be sure to credit him in my post-tournament speech.

With that, I headed off down the fairway, past the crossing I'd manned on Saturday morning, past the drunks and millionaires in the hospitality suites, and towards the grandstand behind the green. Earlier in the week I'd noticed a small bridge down there – a perfect spot to watch all the action, especially as the Sunday pin position was tucked in the back corner.

When I got there it was unmanned, although there was a stern-faced middle-aged woman in a marshal's uniform hanging around who clearly hadn't got the memo

I'd sent about not taking the job too seriously.

'Where the bloody hell do you think you're going?' she barked, stomping over towards me as I parked my backside on the knee-high wall that ran along one side of the bridge.

'Nowhere,' I replied with unintended precision. I sounded calmer than I felt.

'Well, you can't sit there. The players have to walk across the bridge to the next tee.'

'Sorry,' I said, almost swallowing the word.

I was about to get up and leave when I noticed her orange armband. She was an ordinary marshal. I pulled my own armband out of my pocket and waved it at her. 'Don't worry about it. I'm going to stay here for a while.'

It was as if I'd placed a garlic tiara on the head of Dracula's granny. She didn't spit or snarl, although for a second I thought she might do both, but barrelled off towards the grandstand in search of someone less senior to harass.

My new vantage point didn't quite offer the

excitement of my perch behind the tee – for one thing, the crowd was herded on the other side of the stream surrounding the green – but the view was perfect. I stayed there for an hour, during which time I saw Montgomerie hole a long putt to go four up on Hoch. I saw Hal Sutton duff a chip across the green and concede the hole to Langer to go four down. I saw a beautifully stroked putt by David Toms lip out, probably because I blew it off track. I was that close. In fact, if I'd climbed into Sergio Garcia's bag I couldn't have felt any closer to the action. Once again I had washed up in golfing nirvana.

Curtis Strange's brother and someone else wearing Team USA armbands sat along the wall from me, close enough for me to hear snatches of their conversation as the matches went through.

'We're fucked,' I overheard one of them say – a remark that might have got him thrown out of the R&A clubhouse but at least had the virtue of accuracy.

By now, the cheers from around the course

were almost continuous. I could just about see a scoreboard through the trees off to the right of the green. It was covered in blue. Europe was up in eight matches, level in two and down in two. Only Scott Verplank and Jim Furyk were ahead for the Americans. Tiger Woods was down to Jesper Parnevik. Even more stunningly, Phil Mickelson was three down against Phillip Price.

The Price–Mickelson match would be coming my way very soon. I had a choice: I could stay and watch what was beginning to look like the biggest shock of the tournament (and of the world number two's life). Alternatively, I could wander over towards the fourteenth and watch Montgomerie finishing off Hoch.

There was a huge roar. It could only be a victory roar. 'What happened?' I asked Curtis's brother, who was listening to his walkie-talkie.

'Montgomerie's won,' he said.

Driving to the course that morning, I had promised myself that if I did nothing else for the rest of my life, I would make sure I was there when the putt that won the Ryder Cup dropped in the hole. I had seen a lot over the last three days but I had also missed enough tournament highlights to keep Sky Sports on the air for a month. Montgomerie's victory was only the latest. It would also be the last. Hopefully.

I decided that I would choose a spot on the course and stay there. The trick was choosing the right spot. Leaving the tenth green, I had a look at the scoreboard. Padraig Harrington had beaten Mark Calcavecchia 5 and 4. That put Europe ahead 10–8. Langer had made it 11–8 when he finished off Hal Sutton on the fifteenth. Toms reduced the gap by sneaking past Garcia on the last, but then Darren Clarke won a half-point against Duval. By my calculations one of three players had a chance of being Europe's match-winning hero – Niclas Fasth, Paul McGinley or Phillip Price – and the chances were that the denouement would take place on the sixteenth green.

Everyone else had made the same

calculation. I could hardly move for the number of people inside the ropes around the green. Outside the ropes, it was Trafalgar Square on New Year's Eve. Big H, the zone captain, was standing over by the seventeenth tee looking very relaxed for a man in charge of a potential scrum.

'The real pandemonium won't start until the matches come through. We'll need to guard the ropes here – make sure people don't run across in front of the tee,' he said, smiling. 'Some hope. Not to worry. Anyway, what have you been up to?'

I shrugged. 'Just running around, trying to see as much as possible. You?'

'Hardly moved from this spot. I've got a sore toe.'

'Oh, really. What happened?' I said with as much sympathy as I could muster.

'Yeah. There were one or two blisters on the side of it at the start of the week. I dressed them when I got home last night but I think I might have to go to the chiropodist . . .'

While Big H and I discussed treatment

options for a severely blistered toe, the Ryder Cup was heading towards a finish.

The area around the sixteenth green was even more crowded by now as the players and caddies from the matches that had finished started to gather. Scott Verplank, one up against Lee Westwood, was just about to putt as I found a spot behind the green next to Billy Foster, Darren Clarke's caddy. I'd known Billy a little when I was a caddy, enough to strike up a conversation. I asked him what the day had been like. 'The best ever,' he whispered. 'I've been in seven Ryder Cups now and this has been the best ever.'

Verplank holed out to keep his lead. Meanwhile, the scoreboard changed: Thomas Bjorn had just beaten Stewart Cink. Europe now needed just two points.

So much was happening, so much changing so quickly, that I was dizzy trying to keep up. Even now, a few months later, I'm dizzy writing about it. I'm sure you're dizzy reading about it, so what I'm going to do is stop, focus and ask you to contemplate this one startling fact: unassuming, modest Phillip Price, Pontypridd Man of the Year 1994, the so-called weakest link of the European team, the man I'm ashamed to say I thought was completely useless, had a 25-foot putt on the sixteenth green to beat Phil Mickelson and win the Ryder Cup for Europe. More importantly, I had an uninterrupted view of the shot.

I could see the ball was on target as soon as he struck it. It rolled towards the centre of the cup and fell in, and so did the heavens. I briefly contemplated pushing through the greenside celebrations to find an attractive golfer's wife to hug but settled instead for slapping Billy Foster on the back. Phillip Price had won the Ryder Cup for Europe and I would spend the next thirty years boring people with the story of how I was there.

Except he hadn't, and I wouldn't. The arithmetic had changed. Over on the eighteenth hole Paul Azinger had holed a bunker shot to win a half-point against Niclas

Fasth. It was now down to the Irishman Paul McGinley to win the cup for Europe. Confused? Me, too. All I knew for certain was that McGinley was standing by the side of the eighteenth green, sizing up a ten-foot putt for the Ryder Cup and I was standing beside the seventeenth tee, with my arms outstretched in a modern reinterpretation of the little Dutch boy with his finger in the dyke.

'Man the ropes!' Big H yelled. 'Stop them walking across the front of the tee.'

Hundreds of people were surging across the fairway in an effort to get to the eighteenth green. I should have been surging with them yet for some inexplicable reason I felt a sudden impulse to start marshalling.

'You can't walk across there,' I said to someone.

'Oh really,' he replied as he walked across there.

Beside me, Phil Mickelson and his wife were sitting on the back of a golf buggy. Curtis Strange was in the driving seat. 'So what needs to happen in order for us to pull it off?' Mickelson said, running his hands through his hair. Strange didn't even turn round, though I could see him silently shaking his head.

The surge turned into a stampede. I was in danger of being run over. All around me marshals were deserting their positions as people flooded past. It was like the fall of Paris. I looked across at Big H. Even he had disappeared, presumably to hide his free marshalling gear and souvenir 'Quiet Please' sign from the looting Nazis.

'Oh, fuck it,' I said to no one in particular.

The eighteenth green was only 600 yards away. The path was blocked by every golf fan who ever was and ever will be but if I could just make it to the fairway rope I would be able to get to the green by running up the side of the fairway. I pulled out my senior marshal's armband and started waving it in the air. No one paid any attention. I could have pulled out a Colt .45 and no one would have paid any attention. Still, I tried to push my way through.

'Excuse me,' I shouted at one particularly stubborn human barricade. 'It's an emergency.'

He turned round, red-faced and sweating and just as frustrated as me. 'Piss off,' he said. Or at least I think he did. My lip-reading isn't what it used to be and his words were engulfed by this enormous sound, like the noise of a coastal village being overwhelmed by a tidal wave.

Paul McGinley had holed his putt. Europe had won the Ryder Cup.

The celebrations began just as soon as Tiger gave Jesper Parnevik a six-foot putt for a half, ending the last of the twelve singles matches. Europe had triumphed by fifteen and a half points to twelve and a half.

McGinley was persuaded that diving into the lake at the front of the eighteenth green on a cold September night was a terrific idea. I even missed that part of the fun, having been dragooned into helping the crowd make its way off the course and towards the bars in the tented village. As if 10,000 celebrating European fans needed my help to find a drink.

Yet amid all this euphoria I felt utterly dejected. I had somehow conspired to miss the Golden Moment. The fact is, I always miss the golden moments. Take me to any football stadium in the world and it is guaranteed I'll be in the toilet when the winning goal is scored. Get me a free pass to the Playboy mansion and I'll ring the doorbell on the day Hugh Hefner turns the place into a Lutheran retreat. It's the sad, pathetic story of my life. My problem is that I have no timing. My other problem, as you might have guessed from the last sentence but one, is that I'm a self pitying malcontent. If I lived in LA I'd get some therapy; I'd join a twelve-step programme and find myself a proper sense of perspective.

Steps one to twelve: so what if I didn't have the memory of seeing McGinley's putt fall into the hole? What about the memories I did have? I'd seen Europe triumph at the Ryder Cup. Thanks to Lee Westwood, I'd seen the greatest golf shot I could ever hope to see. I'd seen Tiger Woods up close. Better still, I'd seen his girlfriend up close. I'd managed to avoid watching the opening ceremony, I'd been given an armful of free golf gear and I was there when Colin Montgomerie actually cracked a joke. Best of all, I'd watched Phillip Price hole a putt to beat Phil Mickelson. No one, except perhaps Monty and Phillip Price, had had a better Ryder Cup than me. Yet as I catalogued the events of the last five days, my thoughts wandered elsewhere, to the conversation I was bound to have when someone found out I'd been at the 2002 Ryder Cup.

'You were? Fantastic. Did you see McGinley hole the winning putt?'

'Afraid not,' I'd have to reply. 'I was standing behind some bloke with a head the size of a Habitat beanbag and didn't see a bloody thing.'

That was it. My mind was made up. I'd just pretend that I was there. Why not? I almost *was* there. In any case, I've been boasting for years about how I saw the Clash play at

Glasgow Apollo the night Joe Strummer was arrested for inciting a riot. In some versions of the story I've even spent the night in the cell with Strummer. The truth was my mother said I couldn't go, that punk rock was a threat to society and, in any case, I had maths homework to do. Yet to this day there are close friends of mine who are under the impression I was one of Scotland's leading punk figureheads, right up there with Big John from the Exploited.

If it worked back then, why not now?

I tried out my revised Ryder Cup story on a friend in the media centre, even embellishing it with a fictional hug I received from McGinley as he walked off the green. It seemed to do the trick, although to be honest my friend was too busy working to notice that the tips of my ears were flashing like the lights on top of a police car.

Next up was the post-tournament party for the marshals.

Actually, it wasn't so much a party as a sit-down with free food and beer. Not that

I'm complaining. Free food and beer at the end of a long but exhilarating day is pretty much my idea of the perfect human experience. I loaded up my plate, grabbed two beers and took a seat next to Steve, my lawyer friend.

'Hey buddy,' he said brightly. 'Where you been? Did you have a good time?'

'The best. The absolute best,' I replied, and I meant it.

'Me too. I was on the eighteenth all day. You?'

'The sixteenth, mostly.'

He shook his head. 'You didn't see McGinley hole the putt?'

'Jesus Christ, of course I did,' I yelled.

He looked startled – justifiably so, given that he'd asked a simple question and I'd responded as if he'd just accused me of sleeping with his wife.

'I was only asking. Is there something wrong?' he said.

Of course there is, you stupid fucking Yank – I missed the Golden Moment.

'No, not at all. Brilliant, wasn't it? The putt, I mean,' I said. 'I was right there. Did I tell you that?'

'Congratulations. You must be a very happy man.'

Two out of two. This was going better than expected. Another five years of telling people I'd seen Paul McGinley win the Ryder Cup for Europe and I'd probably end up believing that I actually did. However, the ultimate test remained.

It's not that my girlfriend hates golf, it's just that she would rather French kiss Dale Winton than watch more than five seconds of it on television. So you can imagine my surprise when I walked through the door after returning from the Belfry and the first thing she said was not 'You're home, darling, I've missed you' but 'Wasn't that absolutely fantastic?'

'Wasn't what fantastic?' I said, bemused.

'The golf. The Ryder Cup,' she said, as if I was the one who was behaving strangely.

I was only through the door and already she was being sarcastic. 'Very funny.'

'No, really,' she said. 'I was supposed to go shopping on Sunday afternoon but I stayed in to watch the singles matches on TV.'

She was serious. 'You're serious?' I said.

'What about Phillip Price?' she said.

One week earlier she thought Phillip Price was the bloke who played opposite Christopher Lee in the Dracula films.

'And Tiger. What's up with that guy? How come he wins all these tournaments on his own and then when it comes to team sports he's crap?'

How come, indeed.

We've been together sixteen years. Wonderful years. I won't bore you with the details of what we've been up to, except to say we have done everything together. Everything except have a conversation like this, about golf; a conversation about golf in which the enthusiasm shown by me was met with similar enthusiasm from her.

'And Paul McGinley. What about that Paul McGinley?' she swooned. 'Did you see his putt?'

I hesitated. Fatally. 'Eh, yes.'

I know this isn't a book about personal relationships but this is probably an appropriate spot to mention that if you've been with someone for sixteen years there's absolutely no point in trying to deceive that person in any way, shape or form. They know you too well. They know that you secretly liked the Spice Girls, they know that if you eat one chocolate biscuit you will eat the entire packet in five minutes. They know that if you're lying you hesitate, blurt out the untruth and then change the subject.

'Anyway, I better get my bag unpacked,' I said.

She laughed and shook her head. 'I don't believe it. You went all the way to the Belfry to watch the Ryder Cup, got a stupid job as a marshal so you could have the best view possible and then you didn't see the putt that won the bloody thing. Unbelievable.'

Sadly, it was entirely believable. I didn't see Paul McGinley hole the putt that won the Ryder Cup for Europe. Guilty as charged, Your Honour.

There was nothing I could say in my defence, so I didn't say anything at all. Instead I bent down, opened up my rucksack and pulled out the small polystyrene paddle I'd managed to steal from the marshals' HQ on the final morning.

'I brought you a present,' I said, handing her my precious 'Quiet Please' sign. 'Come to think of it, it's not really a present, it's a suggestion. I'm begging you – don't tell a soul.'

But it was too late. She was already on the phone. 'Lawrence is back from the Ryder Cup,' I heard her say. 'And you'll never guess what the idiot didn't see . . .'